W9-BUY-344

SIGNS IN CONTEMPORARY CULTURE

ANNENBERG/LONGMAN COMMUNICATION BOOKS
George Gerbner and Marsha Siefert, Editors
The Annenberg School of Communications
University of Pennsylvania, Philadelphia

Arthur Asa Berger
San Francisco State University

SIGNS IN CONTEMPORARY CULTURE

An Introduction to Semiotics

Illustrations by the author

Longman
New York & London

SIGNS IN CONTEMPORARY CULTURE
An Introduction to Semiotics

Longman Inc., 1560 Broadway, New York, N.Y. 10036
Associated companies, branches, and representatives
throughout the world.

Developmental Editor: Gordon T. R. Anderson
Production/Manufacturing: Ferne Y. Kawahara
Composition: Graphicraft Typesetters
Printing and Binding: Malloy Lithographing Inc.

Library of Congress Cataloging in Publication Data
Berger, Arthur Asa, Date.
  Signs in contemporary culture.

  (Annenberg/Longman communication books)
  Bibliography: p.
  Includes index.
  1. Signs and symbols. 2. Semiotics. I. Title. II. Series.
P99.B437   1984   001.51   83–17529
ISBN 0–582–28487–2

Manufactured in the United States of America
Printing: 9 8 7 6 5 4 3 2 1   Year: 92 91 90 89 88 87 86 85 84

The voice is the voice of Jacob
But the hands are the hands of Esau
(Gen. 27:22)

Contents

Preface   ix

Acknowledgments   xi

1   Definition   1
Honor in Shakespeare's Henry IV, Part I   5

2   How Signs Work   9
Sherlock Holmes   16

3   Signs, Symbols, and Signals   19
Empire of Signs   21

4   Forms of Signs   24
Eight Hypotheses on Digital Watches   29

5   Visual Aspects of Signs   33
The Judy Chicago Show   38

6   Problems of Signs   42
Pop Art   45

7   Denotation and Connotation   48
Comics and Ideology   51

8   Imaginary Signs   57
Freud on Dreams   62

9   Signs that Lie   67
On Parody   71

10   Men's Looks: Signifiers and Life-Style   75
Denimization   80

11   Coherence in Signs   83
Formulas in the Public Arts   85

12   Who Uses Signs?   89
Poetry as Sign   92

13   Signs and Identity   95
The Rewards of Myth   104

14   Terms Associated with Signs   108
Auteur *Criticism*   111

15   Signs and Images   114
Photography   119

16   No Sign as Sign   122
The Natural Look   124

17   Signs that Confound   127
Arcimboldo   130

18   Sign Modifiers   133
Cartooning   136

19   Manifest and Latent Meaning in Signs   139
Robinson Crusoe   143

20   Analyzing Signs and Sign Systems   148
"Reach Out and Touch Someone"   151

21   Codes   155
Baseball   162

22   Characteristics of Codes   165
Foods as Signs   170

23   Meaning   173
"The Paper Chase"   177

References   181

A Selected Bibliography   184

Dictionary of Concepts   189

Index   193

Preface

This book is an introduction to semiotic or semiological thought and an application of semiotics to the mass media, the arts, and related concerns. It is designed for the general reader who has no background in semiotics, although I believe that even those with a familiarity with the subject may find it useful. *Signs in Contemporary Culture*, unlike many other semiotics books, is as much concerned with the uses of semiotic theory as it is with the theory itself.

Each chapter is divided into two sections: the first deals with a theoretical topic or topics from semiotics and the second applies a concept from the theoretical section to some aspect of the mass media. Every theoretical section has an application which is meant to suggest how semiotics can be used to understand better the mass media, popular culture, and everyday life.

Semiotics, the "science of signs" and of the codes used to understand them, is an "imperialistic" science, one which has applicability to many different areas of life. (Some semioticians go so far as to claim that it is a master discipline which can be used to explain every aspect of communication.) Thus, in this book you will find discussions of such topics as comics, detective fiction, humor, formulaic genres, advertising, sports, photography, fashion, television programs, cartoons, theatre, artifacts, videogames, fairy tales, films, and corporate symbols. The concepts found in semiotics can be used to explicate these topics and many others, as you will soon discover.

Actually, we are all semioticians, even if we don't recognize it or understand the technicalities of the subject. (We are all like the character in the Molière play who never realized that he always spoke prose.) We all know about status symbols; we all talk about "images"; and we all read articles in newspapers and magazines about "body language" and "dressing for power." We all practice semiotics on a very superficial level and in a most unsystematic way, as one might expect from untutored and unconscious semioticians.

Signs in Contemporary Culture is meant to help you become more systematic and more rigorous semioticians. There is a catch that I must mention, however. Semiotics is a very complicated science. It has its own terminology and in order to function as a semiotician you will have to learn *some* of this language. So you will find yourself dealing with terms such as signifiers and signifieds, codes, icons, and indexes. I have kept this arcane terminology to a minimum and, since this is an introduction to the subject, avoided certain areas of controversy (among semioticians).

I have provided an annotated bibliography at the end of the book for those who wish to pursue the subject further. There is a large and rapidly growing literature on the subject and many of the books cited in the bibliography contain large bibliographies themselves. I hope, also, that readers of *Signs in Contemporary Culture* will be able to use semiological and semiotic concepts to make their own analyses of our mass-mediated culture, that they will find semiotics a key that unlocks all kinds of doors and offers insights and understanding that are not available to those without a familiarity with the subject.

Signs in Contemporary Culture is a personal (perhaps even idiosyncratic) explanation of semiotic and semiological theory and application of this theory to the mass media, popular culture, the arts, and culture in general. Charles Sanders Peirce, one of the founding fathers of the subject, once said "...this universe is perfused with signs, if it is not composed exclusively of signs." If this is the case, and I believe it is, it makes sense for us to understand what signs are and how they function and to explore some of the more interesting and revealing signs about us.

Acknowledgments

I owe a special debt of gratitude to George Gerbner, who saw a prototype of this book and urged me to expand it into a full-length text. I am also grateful for his and Marsha Siefert's editorial advice and encouragement. They were good enough to provide me with two reviewers, whose comments and suggestions were of inestimable value. I appreciate the close readings they gave my manuscript and their many helpful ideas.

I also benefitted from the ideas (and in some cases the friendship) of the following people: Umberto Eco, Jean-Marie Benoist, Roland Barthes, Jonathan Culler, Ferdinand de Saussure, Charles Sanders Peirce, Fustel de Coulanges, Johan Huizinga, Stanley Milgram, Claude Cossette, Claude Lévi-Strauss, Ernest Dichter, Vladimir Propp, Aaron Wildavsky, Mircea Eliade, Mary Douglas, Irving Louis Horowitz, Alan Dundes, William Fry, Terence Hawkes, Robert Scholes, Rosalind Coward, Frederic Jameson, Keir Elam, John Ellis, Alan Gowans, Ed Graham, Edgar Morin, David Noble, Seymour Chatman, Jean Piaget, Jean Guenot, Marshall McLuhan, Thomas Sebeok, and Gregory Bateson. There were many others. Thanks, also, to Jan Browman for some fine photos.

One

Definition

Signs are things which stand for other things or, to add a different dimension to the matter, *anything that can be made to stand for something else.* As C. S. Peirce put it, a sign "is something which stands to somebody for something in some respect or capacity." (1958,2:228) Among the most important kinds of signs are words. The *word* "tree," and what it stands for, "a woody perennial plant having a single usually elongate main stem generally with few or no branches on its lower part," are not the same. The word is used as a sign of the idea or concept. And there is an intent to communicate that must also be kept in mind. Signs "mean" something. What they mean, how they generate meaning, how we use signs—these questions are what this book is about.

Words are not the only kinds of signs. Think of a theatrical presentation. There is scenery: canvas and other materials give the illusion of a tropical forest or a Victorian drawing room. There is costuming. The costumes suggest, to the audience, a certain mood and life-style. (In the old westerns, for example, heroes wore white and villains wore black, so you had no trouble knowing who to root for.) Then there are the actors and actresses, who are people pretending to be certain characters feeling certain emotions. The performers achieve this end by appropriating the signs of their characters. They use certain mannerisms, gestures, language, and so on to approximate the signs of the emotions they are supposedly feeling. If the performers are good at their work they deceive the audience (which makes a "willing suspension of disbelief") and trick the audience into having certain emotional responses.

It is all done, not with mirrors, but with signs. As an example of the use of signs let us consider professional wrestling. This kind of wrestling is not a sport but, technically, an "exhibition." In truth it is a theatrical performance embedded in a pseudo-sport, and one which generates incredible excitement in the audiences that attend these events. In his essay "The World of Wrestling" (which appeared in *Mythologies*) Roland Barthes discusses some of the important signs which inform wrestling.

He discusses "the drenching and vertical quality of the flood of light" in wrestling and suggests that "'wrestling partakes of the nature of the great solar spectacles, Greek drama and bull-fights; in both, a light without shadow generates an emotion without reserve." (1972:15) Thus the

Photograph by Jan Browman

Wrestling is a form of popular theatre that really should have more work done on it by scholars and students of the public arts.

lighting in wrestling, as in all dramatic presentations, is of crucial importance and has a profound effect on the emotional responses of the viewers
of these presentations. (As Herbert Zettl puts it in *Sight, Sound, Motion*,
"Light, like music, can evoke a great variety of specific feelings with us.
Lighting alone may not be able to make us cry or laugh...but it can
certainly indicate to us whether the scene reflects a bright and gay or a
mysterious and ominous mood." [1973:29])

Barthes also discusses the builds of wrestlers. "The physique of the
wrestlers, therefore, constitutes a basic sign, which like a seed contains the
whole fight." (1972:18) In this respect he mentions an infamous French
wrestler Thauvin:

> a fifty-year old with an obese and sagging body, whose type of asexual
> hideousness always inspires feminine nicknames, displays in his flesh the
> characters of baseness, for his part is to represent what, in the classical concept
> of the *salaud*, "the bastard" (the key-concept of any wrestling-match), appears
> as organically repugnant. (1972:17)

Thauvin's body is, Barthes tells us, a sign of ugliness and baseness...and
this explains why Thauvin is known to the French public as *la barbaque*—
"stinking meat."

What is crucial, Barthes explains, is that the signs in wrestling have an
absolute clarity about them so that wrestling does a wonderful job of
providing the French public with what it wants, "...the image of passion,
not passion itself." That, of course, is what theater does as well so that
Barthes' essay on wrestling may be read a semiological analysis of theatre,
using one form of theatre, professional wrestling, for its subject matter.

The systematic study of signs is known as semiology, which means,
literally, "words about signs." The *semi* in semiology comes from the
Greek term *sēmeîon*, sign. Semiologists look at signs both as "things in
themselves" (Thauvin's body) and as "signs" or indicators of other things
(Thauvin's physical ugliness reflects his moral ugliness). There is an
elaborate and arcane language that semiologists have developed to analyze
signs; we don't have to use all the concepts they use but we can adopt a
number of them and do a pretty good job of understanding signs.

Let me quote, now, a passage from one of the founding fathers of sign
analysis, the Swiss linguist Ferdinand de Saussure. He wrote in his *Course
in General Linguistics*:

> Language is a system of signs that expresses ideas, and is therefore comparable
> to a system of writing, the alphabet of deaf-mutes, symbolic rites, polite
> formulas, military signals, etc. But it is the most important of all these systems.
>
> *A science that studies the life of signs within society* is conceivable; it would be
> part of social psychology and consequently of general psychology; I shall call it

semiology (from Greek *sēmeîon* "sign"). Semiology would show what constitutes a sign, what laws govern them. (1966:16)

This is one of the charter statements of semiology, a statement which opens up the study of almost every aspect of communication to us.

For a slightly different approach let us consider Umberto Eco's statement in *A Theory of Semiotics*:

> Semiotics is concerned with everything that can be taken as a sign. A sign is everything which can be taken as significantly substituting for something else. This something else does not necessarily have to exist or to actually be somewhere at the moment in which a sign stands for it. Thus semiotics is in principle the discipline studying everything which can be used in order to lie. If something cannot be used to tell a lie, conversely it cannot be used to tell the truth; it cannot in fact be used "to tell" at all. I think that the definition of a "theory of the lie" should be taken as a pretty comprehensive program for a general semiotics. (1976:7)

The fact that signs have a double valence and can mislead or "lie" in addition to being truthful gives them great power and makes them rather complicated phenomena with which to deal.

In this application we concern ourselves with one of the most important kinds of signs—words, and, in particular, the word "honor." Is "honor" just a word? And is a word just "air," as Falstaff argues?

HAL AND FALSTAFF AND THE PROBLEM OF HONOR

One of the more interesting aspects of Shakespeare's *Henry IV, Part I* is the way in which honor is handled. The play deals with a number of topics and has a number of themes: the education of a king, Hal's search for a father, his calculating and cold intelligence, and so on, but of chief interest here is the matter of how honor is treated. Shakespeare may not have read any of the semiologists, but he certainly understood the subject.

When the play opens, Hal's father, the king, is bemoaning the "fact" that his son is a wastrel, and is comparing Hal to Hotspur, Northumberland's son. The King says, discussing Hotspur's triumphs on the battlefield:

> Yes, there thou mak'st me sad, and maks't me sin
> In envy that my Lord Northumberland
> Should be the father to so blest a son,
> A son who is the theme of honor's tongue,
> Amongst a grove the very straightest plant
> Who is sweet fortune's minion and her pride;
> Whilst I, by looking on the praise of him,
> See riot and dishonor stain the brow
> Of my young Harry.
>
> (1962:7, 8)

The king then says he wishes it could be proved that his son and Hotspur had been exchanged in the crib.

Of course, being "the theme of honor's tongue," which suggests having an excellent reputation, is not exactly the same thing as being honorable—though Hotspur, as his name suggests, is both excitable ("hot") and honorable, in a way that will be explained by the clown-figure Falstaff shortly. So we start with a comparison and one that is odious, like most comparisons. And we are left with the question of whether "honor's tongue," or reputation, is the same thing as honor.

In the second scene we discover something rather interesting—that Hal is not really a drunk and wastrel but only pretending to be one. He explains why in the speech that follows:

> Yet herein will I imitate the sun
> Who doth permit the base contagious clouds
> To smother up his beauty from the world,
> That, when he please again to be himself,
> Being wanted, he may be more wondered at
> By breaking through the foul and ugly mists
> Of vapors that did seem to strangle him.
> If all the year were playing holidays
> To sport would be as tedious as to work:
> But when they seldom come, they wished-for come,
> And nothing pleaseth but rare accidents.
> So, when this loose behavior I throw off
> And pay the debt I never promised,
> How much better than my word I am,
> By so much shall I falsify men's hopes;
> And like bright metal on a sullen ground,
> My reformation, glitt'ring o'er my fault,
> Shall show more goodly and attract more eyes
> Than that which hath no foil to set it off.
> I'll so offend to make offense a skill
> Redeeming time when men think least I will.
>
> (1962:14, 15)

Hal's reformation will seem more remarkable and wonderful, he points out, after he's established a reputation as a ne'er-do-well. Furthermore, by playing the drunk, Hal is putting people off their guard. They expect little of him and thus can be defeated more easily. Hal is a calculating person; we learn this from his speech. We also learn that he is a counterfeit or, from the semiological perspective, one who "lies" with signs. He's also a rather profound psychologist who recognizes that it is differences which are crucial in life. Holidays are meaningful only because they are interruptions from the normal course of events.

We can contrast Prince Hal's approach to life with Hotspur's. The latter's attitude toward honor is very different—it is romantic and super-

heroic at best and foolhardy at worst. We see this is his speech in Act I
Scene 3:

> By heaven, methinks it were an easy leap
> To pluck bright honor from the pale-faced moon,
> Or dive into the bottom of the deep,
> Where fathom-line could never touch the ground,
> And pluck up drowned honor by the locks
> So he that doth redeem her thence might wear
> Without corrival all her dignities.
>
> (1962:21, 22)

Hotspur has a wild imagination and an enormous amount of self-
confidence; it might also be described as arrogance or foolhardiness.
Notice the difference between the oppositions in Hal's speech and Hotspur's. Hal is pretending to be degenerate so he'll fool his enemies and
appear more glorious when he assumes his true role. Hotspur, on the other
hand, is willing to fly up to the moon or dive down to the deepest depths of
the sea to "pluck" honor and gain fame.

There is another important scene in which Hal discusses honor, in Act
III, Scene 2, when Hal explains to his father, the king, what's really been
going on. His father has just called him a degenerate who cannot be
trusted. The prince answers, saying:

> Do not think so. You shall not find it so.
> And God forgive them that so much have swayed
> Your majesty's good thoughts away from me.
> I will redeem all this on Percy's head,
> And in the closing of some glorious day
> Be bold to tell you that I am your son,
> When I will wear a garment all of blood,
> And stain my favors in a bloody mask,
> Which, washed away, shall scour my shame with it.
> And that shall be the day, whene'er it lights,
> That this same child of honor and renown,
> This gallant Hotspur, this all-praised knight
> And your unthought-of Harry chance to meet.
>
> (1962:64, 65)

When Prince Hal and Hotspur (Percy) do meet, Hal kills Hotspur and
redeems himself. The confrontation between the "unthought-of" Harry
and the "all-praised" knight is, once more, one of opposites and Harry's
triumph, in such circumstances, becomes more significant.

The final disquisition on honor is to come from Falstaff, the fat old
drunkard and clown and, not incidentally, one of the greatest comic figures
in all literature. Falstaff is a prodigious drinker and eater but, above all, he

is a supreme realist. His speech on the subject of honor is one of the most wonderful passages in the play and one that literary scholars and philosophers have found particularly interesting.

In Act V, Scene 2, Hal and Falstaff are having a conversation about a forthcoming battle and Hal tells Falstaff, half-seriously, that he owes God a death. To which Falstaff replies:

> Tis not due yet: I would be loath to pay him before his day. What need I be so forward with him that calls not on me? Well, 'tis no matter; honor pricks me on. Yea, but how if honor prick me off when I come on? How then? Can honor set a leg? No. Or an arm? No. Or take away the grief of a wound? No. Honor hath no skill in surgery then? No. What is honor? A word. What is that word honor? Air. A trim reckoning! Who hath it? He that dies a Wednesday. Doth he feel it? No. Doth he hear it? No. 'Tis insensible then? Yea, to the dead. But will [it] not live with the living? No. Why? Detraction will not suffer it. Therefore I'll none of it. Honor is a mere scutcheon—and so ends my catechism. (1962:89)

What is honor but a word, and what is a word but air: that is Falstaff's conclusion from his inquiry into honor, its role in society, and related matters. Notice Falstaff's line of inquiry. He asks what honor can do for the wounded soldier and concludes that it can do nothing. "It has no skill in surgery" and, by implication, in life in general. All that honor, a mere word, air, does is lead people to get themselves killed in battle. But when they are dead they cannot enjoy their honor. So honor is a mere "scutcheon" or desire for reputation which is dangerous to one's health and well-being.

We find, then, three approaches to the concept of honor in the play. Hotspur's is the most simple-minded and direct. Honor is something to be gained by outstanding feats or great heroism. It is a prize to be "plucked" and he has no doubt that he is capable of gaining honor and renown. With Hal the matter is more complicated. He prizes honor but he is extremely calculating and perhaps even deceitful in the way he goes about attaining it. Does this behavior tarnish the honor he gains? Is Hal shrewd and clever or something worse? Arguments can be made for both cases. Falstaff, on the other hand, rejects honor (and this shortly after he has said "Honor pricks me on.") Honor is only a word and words are only air. Is Falstaff a realist here, or is he rationalizing his own cowardice? If honor is only a word, what about love, justice, equality, trust? Falstaff may be a drunken sensualist and a coward, but in his disquisition on honor he poses a problem of considerable importance, one that everyone, at some time or other, must come to grips with.

Two

How Signs Work

I said earlier that signs are anything that can be used to stand for something else. But how do signs actually work? There are two important approaches to the sign that I would like to explain. The first is based on an insight from Saussure, who said that signs are composed of two elements—a sound-image (such as a word or visual representation) and a concept for which the sound-image stands:

> I call the combination of a concept and a sound-image a *sign*, but in current usage the term generally designates only a sound-image, a word used for example (*arbor*, etc.). One tends to forget that *arbor* is called a sign only because it carries the concept "tree," with the result that the idea of the sensory part implies the idea of the whole.

> Ambiguity would disappear if the three notions involved here were designated by three names, each suggesting and opposing the others. I propose to retain the word sign (signe) to designate the whole and to replace *concept* and *sound-image* respectively by *signified* (*signifié*) and *signifier* (*signifiant*); the last two terms have the advantage of indicating the opposition that separates them from each other and from the whole of which they are parts. (1966:67)

Sausure used the following diagrams to illustrate his ideas (1966:66–67):

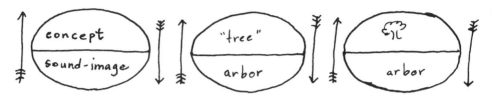

From Ferdinand de Saussure, *A Course in General Linguistics*, New York, McGraw-Hill, 1966. Reprinted with permission of Philosophical Library Publishers.

The next diagram suggests the unity of sign, signifier and signified. Saussure said that signs were like pieces of paper; one side was the signifier, the other side was the signified, and the paper itself, the sign.

SIGN	
Signifier	Signified
Sound-Image	Concept

We cannot separate the signifier and signified from the sign itself. The signifier and signified *form* the sign.

There is one more point that is crucial. For Saussure the relationship between the signifier and signified is *arbitrary*, a matter of chance and convention. This does not mean, Saussure tells us, "that the choice of the signifier is left entirely to the speaker" but rather that it is "unmotivated, i.e. arbitrary in that it actually has no *natural* connection with the signified." (1966:69) [my italics]*

One has to learn what words mean and what signs mean (except in certain cases, which I will explain shortly). In the case of words we have dictionaries which give us the conventional meaning of words; in the case of signs it is often a different story. We generally have to be taught signs, in one way or another. Think, for example, of learning what highway signs

* *Note*: There is some disagreement about the arbitrary nature of the sign. In Peirce's theory, not all signs are arbitrary—only symbols are arbitrary or nonmotivated.

Tips for
Energy Savers

U.S. Department of Energy
Washington, D.C. 20585

mean, driving signals, and so on. We send for a booklet from the Department of Motor Vehicles and learn how various signs are to be interpreted. They are not always self-evident by any means, though in many cases meaning can be understood by interpreting diagrams and pictures.

Let us now turn to the second important approach to understanding signs, a system of sign analysis developed by one of America's most brilliant and neglected thinkers, the philosopher Charles Sanders Peirce (1839–1914). Peirce said signs are related to objects by resembling them, being causally connected to them, or being conventionally tied to them. He used the term *iconic* for resemblance, *indexical* for causal connection, and *symbol* for conventional association. The following chart makes this more clear.

Peirce's Icon/Index/Symbol Trichotomy

Sign	Icon	Index	Symbol
Signify by:	Resemblance	Causal connection	Convention
Examples:	Pictures	Smoke/Fire	Words
	Statues of great figures	Symptom/Disease	Gestures
	Photo of Reagan	(Red spots/Measles)	
Process	Can see	Can figure out	Must learn

This chart is derived from Peirce's statement that:

> an analysis of the essence of a sign...leads to a proof that every sign is determined by its object, either first, by partaking in the characters of the object, when I call the sign an *Icon*; secondly, by being really and in its individual existence connected with the individual object, when I call the sign an *Index*; thirdly, by more or less approximate certainty that it will be interpreted as denoting the object, in consequence of a habit (which term I use as including a natural disposition), when I call the sign a *Symbol*. (Quoted in J. Jay Zeman, "Peirce's Theory of Signs" in T. Sebeok, *A Perfusion of Signs*, 1977:36).

If Saussure's statement about signifiers and signifieds is the key to the semiological mode of analysis, Peirce's trichotomy is the key to semiotic analysis. Both are concerned with signs and signification, but they have different perspectives.

Scholars who use the Saussurean perspective and adopt his essentially linguistic frame of reference in analyzing films, television programs, fashion, and so on, generally identify themselves as semiologists. Those who use Peirce's icon/index/symbol schema identify themselves as semioticians. My own inclination is to use both systems whenever possible since each has utility. For all practical purposes I will consider semiology and semiotics to be essentially similar—since they are both concerned with signification—and will use whichever term I think most appropriate for the thing being analyzed.

Note: There are, Saussure notes, two objections frequently made to his assertion that the relation between the signifier and signified is arbitrary. The first is the matter of *onomatopoeia*. He says that onomatopoeic formations "are never organic elements of a linguistic system" and are not only limited in number but also "chosen somewhat arbitrarily, for they are only approximate and more or less conventional imitations of certain sounds." (1966:69) Also these words evolve and change like other words. The second objection, concerning *interjections*, he dismisses out of hand since interjections have "no fixed bond between their signified and their signifier." (1966:69).

Peirce differs from Saussure on the arbitrariness of signs. For Peirce, indexical relations and iconic relations are natural. Thus smoke is not merely "conventionally" associated with fire, and iconic representations are, obviously, motivated. Only symbols are unmotivated.

Let us move from theory to practice by considering a rather bizarre form of humor that developed in the early 1950s, Roger Price's *droodles*. They are simple drawings that lend themselves to varied (and comic) interpretations. One of Price's more entertaining droodles follows:

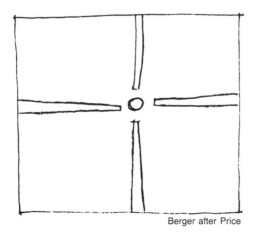

Berger after Price

This droodle was interpreted by Price three different ways:

1. Four elephants inspecting a grapefruit.
2. Crisis in a pool hall.
3. Four unsportsmanlike gopher hunters.

The inventive reader, of course, might find other humorous ways of making "sense" of this drawing. The droodle, which seems to be a combination of doodle and drawing, has two characteristics: first, it is very simple, with very little information given; and second, it is ambiguous and can have many different "meanings."

Semiologically we would say that droodles are signifiers that can have many different signifieds. It is the ingenuity that Price showed in thinking up zany signifieds which generated much of the humor. (It might also be asserted that it is the power of the sign to "lie" that is at the heart of the droodle.) The droodle also plays upon the need we all have to find meaning in things, even when very little data is given.

For our second illustration, consider a humorous drawing I made to illustrate an article in *The Journal of Communication.* (Winter 1981:169.)

The article was on electronic banking and my problem was to find some way of signifying that concept or topic. After a considerable amount of thinking I did the following drawing:

Arthur Asa Berger

From "Electronic Banking and the Death of Privacy," *Journal of Communication*, Winter 1981, p. 169. Reprinted with permission.

The drawing uses iconic and symbolic components to make its point. It merges the "piggy bank" and the electric plug (attached to the tail) to suggest electronic banking. The body of the pig and the pig's tail, which is turned into an electric plug, are both iconic; that is, they both resemble pigs, on the one hand, and electric plugs, on the other. But a pig, with a slot on the top to deposit money, is symbolic. You have to know about piggy banks to make sense of the drawing. The slot on the top turns a drawing of a pig that is iconic into a piggy bank, the meaning of which comes from experience and is symbolic.

Finally, let us look at the Torah, the first five books of the Old Testament. Here we come across God's instruction to the Jews about the significance of circumcision. I quote here from The Jewish Publication Society of America's translation:

God further said to Abraham, "As for you, you and your offspring to come throughout the ages shall keep My covenant. Such shall be the convenant between Me and you and your offspring to follow which you shall keep: every male among you shall be circumcised. You shall circumcise the flesh of your foreskin, and that shall be the sign of the covenant between Me and you. And throughout the generations, every male among you shall be circumcised at the age of eight days." (Gen. 17:9–12)

Circumcision amongst Jews is, then, a sign of the covenant between God and the Jews. It is not always a sign of Jewishness since some non-Jews are circumcised and there are Jewish males from nonobservant families who are not circumcised. But for the Jews, the significance of circumcision is quite clear.

Here I advance the thesis that Sherlock Holmes is really a practicing semiologist and that our fascination with him is connected to the ingenious way in which he applies semiology to problems he faces.

SHERLOCK HOLMES: MASTER SEMIOTICIAN/SEMIOLOGIST*

One of the greatest appeals of Sherlock Holmes is his ability to find meaning where there seems to be nothing. He is, like most of the great detectives (of the classical, deductive school) a master semiotician, who understands signs and what they can tell to the one who knows how to "read" them. One of the more interesting examples of Holmes's ability to interpret phenomena comes in one of his more celebrated cases, "The Blue Carbuncle."

The story begins with Watson visiting Holmes several days after Christmas (to wish him well) and finding Holmes examining a "very seedy and disreputable hard felt hat, much the worse for wear, and cracked in several places." The hat had been recovered by a policeman on Christmas who found a group of young toughs attacking a man carrying a goose. The toughs knocked the hat off the man, who swung his cane to protect himself and broke a window. When the man saw the policeman, he dropped the goose and also fled—leaving the hat and the goose.

Holmes says the hat should not be looked upon as just an old hat but rather as an "intellectual problem." He then asks Watson what he can deduce from the hat about its wearer.

Holmes says, "Here is my lens. You know my methods. What can you gather yourself as to the individuality of the man who has worn this article?" Here is Watson's description of the hat:

* After I wrote this section I discovered a wonderful essay on the semiotic aspects of Holmes's work. See Thomas A. Sebeok and Jean Umiker-Sebeok, "You Know My Method: A Juxtaposition of Charles S. Peirce and Sherlock Holmes," *Semiotica* 26, nos. 3–4 (1979).

I took the tattered object in my hands, and turned it over rather ruefully. It was a very ordinary black hat of the usual round shape, hard, and much the worse for wear. The lining had been of red silk, but was a good deal discoloured. There was no maker's name; but, as Holmes had remarked, the initials "H.B." were scrawled upon one side. It was pierced in the brim for a hat-securer, but the elastic was missing. For the rest, it was cracked, exceedingly dusty, and spotted in several places, although there seemed to have been some attempt to hide the discoloured patches by smearing them with ink. (Doyle, 1975:159–160)

Other facts made known in the story are that the hat was large, hair ends were stuck to the lower end of the lining, there were brown dust and wax stains on the hat, it hadn't been brushed in weeks, and there was a good deal of moisture on the hatband. "I see nothing," Watson says. "On the contrary, Watson, you can see everything. *You fail, however, to reason from what you see. You are too timid in drawing your inferences.*" Watson stands, here, for the typical reader of detective fiction who is given a great deal of information (clues) but is unable to interpret them, neglects them, or misinterprets them. That is why the denouement of mystery stories is so exciting: we are finally shown how neglectful we were and discover that all the information we needed to solve the mystery was given to us. Now let us see all the information Holmes is able to find in the hat:

He picked it up and gazed at it in the peculiar introspective fashion which was characteristic of him. "It is perhaps less suggestive than it might have been," he remarked, "and yet there are a few inferences which are very distinct, and a few others which represent at least a strong balance of probability. That the man was highly intellectual is of course obvious upon the face of it, and also that he was fairly well-to-do within the last three years, although he has now fallen upon evil days. He had foresight, but has less now than formerly, pointing to a moral retrogression, which, when taken with the decline in his fortunes, seems to indicate some evil influence, probably drink, at work upon him. This may account also for the obvious fact that his wife has ceased to love him...He has, however, retained some degree of self-respect," he continued, disregarding my remonstrance. "He is a man who leads a sedentary life, goes out little, is out of training entirely, is middle-aged, has grizzled hair which he has had cut within the last few days, and which he anoints with lime-cream. These are the more patent facts which are to be deduced from his hat. Also, by the way, that it is extremely improbable that he has gas laid on in his house." (1975:160)

To all this Watson replies, "You are certainly joking, Holmes." Holmes then proceeds to show Watson how he arrived at his conclusions, a classic example of semiotic analysis at work.

To simplify matters let me offer a chart which lists the characteristics (or signifieds) and offers the explanations (or signifiers).

Holmes' Semiotic Analysis of the Hat in "The Blue Carbuncle"

Characteristics of the Man Signifieds	Reasoning Behind the Deductions Signifiers
Man was intellectual	Cubic capacity of the hat. "A man with so large a brain must have something in it."
Decline in fortunes	Hat is three years old, of best quality, with ribbed silk bank and excellent lining. But the man hasn't been able to afford a new one.
Foresight	Man had a hat-securer put on hat by special order since hats don't come with them.
Moral retrogression	Broken elastic on hat-securer and hasn't replaced it.
Recent haircut	Hair ends, clean cut by the scissors of a barber, stuck to lower end of hat lining.
Uses lime-cream	Smell of lining.
Goes out little	Dust on hat is brown housedust, not gray street dust, so hung up most of the time.
Wife stopped loving him	Hat hasn't been brushed for weeks.
Out of training	Much moisture . . . perspiration indicates not in good shape.
No gas in the house	Wax stains from candles suggest he reads by candlelight and doesn't have gas.

Watson's reply to all this is "ingenious," and so it is.

After Holmes explains his reasoning, it all seems very simple and quite reasonable. Watson saw everything that Holmes did but Watson paid no attention to all the signs that were presented to him, in part because *he thought* that what he saw was trivial and of no importance. What Watson lacked was methodology (semiotics, semiology) and an appreciation of the importance of seemingly insignificant phenomena. What semiology does is to take the matter of sign interpretation, which is nothing new, and make it more systematic and scientific. Because signs may lie and because the relationship that exists between a signifier and signified is arbitrary, interpreting signs involves a good deal of skill. Holmes is a good example for us; he shows how much there is to see and know if we only can learn how to look.

Three

Signs, Symbols, and Signals

I have defined a sign as something that can be used to stand for something else. We have also discovered that signs can be used to lie. Now I will discuss two related phenomena, symbols and signals, which are subclasses of signs.

A symbol, from the Saussurean perspective, is a kind of sign in which the relationship between the signifier and signified is quasi-arbitrary. And, historical connections of consequence affect our understanding. Saussure explains the matter as follows:

> One characteristic of the symbol is that it is never wholly arbitrary; it is not empty, for there is a rudiment of a natural bond between the signifier and the signified. The symbol of justice, a pair of scales, could not be replaced by just any other symbol, such as a chariot. (1966:68)

A blindfolded goddess holding these scales is an even more powerful symbol of justice, for it intensifies the notion of impartiality and equal treatment which we associate with justice. This figure is a conventional symbol of justice in the Judaeo-Christian western world. There is, then, a logical connection between scales and the concept of justice, but we must still learn to associate the scales and justice. Seeing a drawing of scales does not automatically make one think of justice. Context is crucial here.

A symbol, from our perspective, is something with cultural significance and resonance. It has the ability to excite, and it has great meaning. As has been pointed out already, the Saussurean view of symbols is that they are conventional: we learn what symbols mean and we associate symbols with all kinds of events, experiences, and so on—many of which have powerful emotional resonance for us and for others. The religious symbol is always at the top of a mountain of historical events, legends, etc., and has the power to call to mind much of this material. The same applies to many other symbols.

This point is eloquently made by Clifford Geertz, who writes, in *The Interpretation of Cultures*:

> Thinking consists not of "happenings in the head" (though happenings there and elsewhere are necessary for it to occur) but of a traffic in what have been called, by G. H. Mead and others—significant symbols—words for the most part but also gestures, drawings, musical sounds, mechanical devices like clocks, or natural objects like jewels—anything, in fact, that is disengaged from its mere actuality and used to impose meaning upon experience. From the point of view of any particular individual, such symbols are largely given. He finds them already current in the community when he is born, and they remain, with some additions, subtractions, and partial alterations he may or may not have had a hand in, in circulation when he dies. (1973:45)

Symbols, then, help us make sense of things; they help us shape our behavior and achieve culture.

Though the symbol may be quasi-motivated, we should not over-emphasize its naturalness. Our understanding of symbols (and other sorts of signs as well) often depends on what we bring to them from our cultural heritage.

A signal, as I understand the term, is a kind of sign which is used to generate a response of some kind. What is important is that there is an understanding among all involved that a given signal leads to a particular action. Thus a gun shot off starts a race or a red light tells drivers to stop their cars. A signal is a signifier that functions as a stimulus which occasions (or should occasion) particular responses.

Roland Barthes's Empire of Signs *is a study of Japan as a "system of signs." Barthes examines various "signs" which reflect important aspects of Japanese culture and discovers some extremely interesting things.*

EMPIRE OF SIGNS

Roland Barthes's *Empire of Signs* was published in France in 1970 but it has only recently been translated into English and made available to the American reading public. *Empire of Signs* is a semiological analysis of Japanese culture and reflects Barthes's fascination (maybe love affair would be more appropriate) with Japan. It is a collection of short essays—some no more than a page or two in length—on various aspects of Japanese culture that caught Barthes's attention.

As Barthes writes in his first chapter, "Faraway":

> The author has never, in any sense, photographed Japan. Rather, he has done the opposite: Japan has starred him with any number of "flashes"; or, better still, Japan has afforded him a situation of writing. This situation is the very one in which a certain disturbance of the person occurs, a subversion of earlier readings, a shock of meaning lacerated, extenuated to the point of its irreplaceable void, without the object's ever ceasing to be significant, desirable. (1982:4)

When Barthes writes that he does not wish to "photograph" Japan he means that he isn't after an all-inclusive, systematic interpretation of Japanese culture. Instead, he deals with "flashes," phenomena that strike his attention, make him curious, and lead him to write.

What does Barthes write about? What strikes his attention and leads to his reflections? Does he write about the great heroes of Japanese history? Is he interested in Japanese literary classics? Does he deal with important social movements and political considerations? Not at all.

Instead, he focuses on what might be called the "commonplace" aspects of Japanese culture, matters that are very much part of everyday life and tend to be taken for granted. Here are some of the topics he deals with: chopsticks, sukiyaki, tempura, pachinko, train stations, packages, popular theatre (Bunraku), bowing and manners, stationery stores, Japanese bodies, eyelids, and so on.

Obviously, Barthes is very selective...but there is a logic to his method. His purpose is to see how each of the topics he considers reveals something interesting and important about Japanese culture and character. Each of these topics is a *sign* in a country he describes as an "empire of signs." Thus he is not interested in tempura as tempura, per se, but rather as an indicator of values and imperatives in Japanese culture. His chapter on tempura is called "The Interstice" and explores the significance of tempura as a reflection of the Japanese aesthetic. He writes:

> *Tempura* is stripped of the meaning we traditionally attach to fried food, which is heaviness. Here flour recovers its essence as scattered flower, diluted so lightly that it forms a milk and not a paste; taken up by the oil, this golden milk is so fragile that it covers the piece of food imperfectly, reveals here a pink of shrimp, there a green of pepper, a brown of eggplant, thus depriving the fry of what constitutes our fritter, which is its sheath, its envelope, its density. (1982:24)

Tempura, then, is not just a kind of food; instead, it is a signifier of immense resonance that illuminates the Japanese mind and sensibility.

It is the lightness, fragility, transparency, crispness, and instantaneousness (tempura is prepared before one's eyes in Japan) that strike Barthes's attention, especially since he can compare it with "frites" in France where deep-fried food in batter has an altogether different significance.

Let me cite another example. Barthes is fascinated by the design of the city of Tokyo which, he tells us, has a center (like Western cities) but the center of which is "empty" (the palace of the Emperor is, he writes, "a site both forbidden and indifferent, a residence concealed beneath foliage, protected by moats, inhabited by an emperor who is never seen, which is to say, literally by no one knows who"). (1982:30) This he contrasts with Western cities, which are always full at the center:

> it is here that the values of civilization are gathered and condensed: spirituality (churches), power (offices), money (banks), merchandise (department stores), language (agoras, cafes, and promenades): to go downtown or to the center-city is to encounter the social "truth," to participate in the proud plenitude of "reality." (1982:30)

A city with a center that is empty is simply astonishing for Barthes and he finds himself continually being excited by what ultimately might be described as the Japanese "aesthetic."

Reading *Empire of Signs* one finds oneself constantly coming upon this aesthetic. Sukiyaki is raw and decentered, tempura is an empty sign, Tokyo has an empty center and its streets have no names, Japanese boxes are often more important than the gifts they contain, Haiku poetry wages a war against "meaning," Japanese mirrors are "empty." Japanese life is exciting and astonishing for Barthes because it is so different and Japanese culture provides him with formidable problems of analysis and interpretation. When Barthes, master of the astonishing insight and prose stylist extraordinaire, came to Japan he found a subject worthy of his powers.

Those familiar with Barthes's work can see that *Empire of Signs* is very similar to *Mythologies* in form as well as content. In both books relatively ordinary matters are used to draw powerful conclusions. Barthes, with his vast erudition and keen eye, was able to "read the universe in a grain of sand," and write extremely interesting and perceptive books about his native France and what was for him a most mysterious Japan.

Barthes was conscious of what he was doing. In the very first paragraph of *Empire of Signs* he tells us that he could imagine a fictive nation and treat it as a novelistic object, but that he can also

> though in no way claiming to represent or to analyze reality itself (these being the major gestures of Western discourse)—isolate somewhere in the world (*faraway*) a certain number of features (a term employed in linguistics), and out of these features deliberately form a system. It is this system which I shall call: Japan. (1982:3)

Semiological analysis has its methodological problems, and Barthes is well aware that his choice of subjects may be attacked by some as arbitrary and misleading. But given his precautions, his reading of Japanese culture remains a powerful and extremely suggestive one.

Four

Forms of Signs

In this chapter, I will consider the various forms that signs take. I have been using the term "sign" in a rather specialized way to this point. Now I would like to deal with the different kinds of signs we find in our daily lives.

1. *Advertising Signs.* In *Webster's Ninth New Collegiate Dictionary* the fifth definition offered of "sign" is "a lettered board or other display used to identify or advertise a place of business."* The crucial aspect of this form of sign is that it has a commercial intent. In contemporary American society (and elsewhere, throughout most of the world) there are a variety of media used for signs: neon, plastic, light bulbs forming words, lettering, and so on.

Often the aesthetic components of the sign are used as indicators of the nature of the establishment. That is, they help establish what is known as "corporate identity." This is done through design elements in the sign, typography, symbolization, etc. A glance at *The Wall Street Journal* reveals

---

* By permission. From Webster's Ninth New Collegiate Dictionary © 1983 by Merriam-Webster, Inc., Publishers of the Merriam-Webster® Dictionaries.

Photograph by Jan Browman

The sign above Ghiradelli Square is now one of the cultural landmarks in San Francisco.

that most corporations have distinctive logos and typographies which are used to create an "image" people will remember.

2. *Objects and Material Culture.* Artifacts and other objects (what anthropologists call "material culture") also convey a great deal of information. Think, for example, of all the signs which a person may present to others: eyeglasses, clothes, jewelry, shoes, purses and wallets, attaché cases or briefcases, and so on. When we place this person in a context we get even more information. We can consider the style of the house or building we find the person in, the furniture the person has, the color of the walls, the kinds of paintings or decoration on the walls, the rugs, the spatiality of the room or apartment, the view, and so on.

All of these phenomena mean something and help us gain an understanding of the person who owns or uses them. In some cases the objects are meant to give us a particular feeling or message. Thus, for example, a lawyer's office, full of books, conservatively decorated, helps us feel secure and in the hands of a person with power (knowledge is power is

The kinds of paintings one has on one's walls are a good indicator of the owner's taste and style. Landscape by Jason Berger.

the message of the books). In other cases, objects reveal things about people that the people are not aware of...or don't want to reveal, consciously. As Milton Sapirstein explained in *Paradoxes of Everyday Life*:

> Another woman, preoccupied with her bowel movements, treated her whole house as though it were a gigantic bathroom. All the walls were bare and white and the curtains were made of some transparent plastic material. Decorative bowls, also white, and rather oddly shaped, rested on every available flat surface. A crowning touch, in which she took great pride, was a small fountain, set up in the wall which had originally held a fireplace. (1955:98)

Sapirstein, a psychiatrist, was discussing what people may reveal about themselves when they decorate their homes.

There are even courses offered in some anthropology departments which deal with "garbage-ology." Students systematically collect and analyze garbage to gain some insights into people's life-styles. Often, what garbage-ologists find in a person's garbage contradicts statements people offer about their tastes and practices. In a television program on this topic, a professor teaching a course mentioned that he had queried a family about its tastes and was told no beer was consumed. A study of that family's garbage showed that several cases of beer were consumed each week.

3. *Activities and Performances.*   Things we do signify a great deal. Think, for instance, of how we perspire when we are under stress or are nervous. In his essay "The Romans in Films" (from *Mythologies*) Barthes investigates the meaning of sweat in the film *Julius Caesar*:

> Like the Roman fringe or the nocturnal plait, sweat is a sign. Of what? Of moral feeling. Everyone is sweating because everyone is debating something within himself; we are here supposed to be in the very locus of tragedy, and it is sweat which has the function of conveying this.... To sweat is to think—which evidently rests on the postulate, appropriate to a nation of businessmen, that thought is a violent, cataclysmic operation, of which sweat is only the most benign symptom. (1957:27–28)

Thus the audiences viewing this film were to understand the internal states of the characters through this powerful sign.

We also signify a great deal by our body language, the gestures we all make (which vary considerably in their meaning from place to place), the way our voices rise when we are excited...I could go on and on. We observe these signs in others and they observe them in us. In certain circumstances this is problematical—when, for example, it is important to mask our inner states, as in the game of poker.

In an article "Communicative Competency Among Poker Players," (*Journal of Communication*, Spring 1980:114), David M. Hiyano discusses the problem of deception in poker:

> Poker players refer to a "tell" (short for "telegraph") to mean an unintended verbal or nonverbal signal which reveals either information about the actual strength of a player's hand, or a player's intention to act. In Ekman and Friesen's terms, a tell is a form of communicative leakage or clue to deception.
>
> The classic, most obvious tells are positive or negative affect displays, such as when amateurs smile, touch their noses, sit up straight when they are ready to bet a strong hand, or slump down in their seats when they have a losing hand. Tells are also indicated by overly strong or hesitant betting movements, general attentiveness, an increase in talking, gaze direction, posture corrections, the use of self and object adaptors, and an overall interest in the hand in play and the size of the pot.

Because poker is a game which combines luck (the draw of the cards) and skill (betting, bluffing, interpreting behavior), good poker players must develop considerable skill in masking their feelings and, at the same time, interpreting the behaviors of others. Professional poker players are masters of faking, leading other players astray (via "false tells") so poker remains an art of performance as much as a game. The central problem among good players is the "bluff," which is a "false tell." It is crucial that an element of indeterminacy be introduced into the game so that competitors cannot automatically equate betting with a strong hand, and that is where the bluff comes in.

Obviously, a bluff is a sign that lies. We will deal with this matter in more detail elsewhere when we consider other areas of life (besides poker) where false tells or misleading signs are used.

4.   *Sound and Music.*   Under this classification I'm including sounds and noises, in general, and music, in particular. Both sound and music are used to generate emotional responses, based on culturally generated associations. In other words, the emotion (signified) and the sound (signifier) have an arbitrary relationship. Some sounds are the aural equivalent of icons—that is, they sound just like the thing being represented. We call these sound effects. Sound and music play an extremely important role in films and television productions. They function as "cues" which indicate how we should respond emotionally to a given action or event. These cues, I would argue, are based on previously learned associations and are not natural.

A student of mine who questioned the arbitrary nature of emotional responses to music performed an experiment in one of my classes. He played selections of music taken from different television programs he had produced and asked members of the class to write down the kinds of feelings the music engendered and the kinds of scenes that the music accompanied. The responses of the members of the class were so varied that it was impossible to establish any connection between a musical passage and a mood or scene.

From the semiological perspective, objects (such as digital watches) are signs. We can analyze the signifying aspects of the object to see what it reflects about the culture in which it is found. Here I offer some speculations about the "meaning of digital watches."

EIGHT HYPOTHESES ON THE SIGNIFICANCE OF DIGITAL WATCHES

We all live in a world of objects—what anthropologists call "material culture." By this they mean things such as our clothes, the foods we eat, the gadgets we use, and so on. Many of these objects may seem to be trivial and not worth thinking about; however, seen as *signs* they point to matters of great significance or importance in the same way that clues point to guilty persons in detective stories. Ernest Dichter, the well-known expert in motivation research, wrote a book called *The Handbook of Consumer Motivations*, the subtitle of which is "The Psychology of the World of Objects."

In this book he suggested that objects have "souls" and wrote:

> The objects which surround us do not simply have utilitarian aspects; rather, they serve as a kind of mirror which reflects our image. Objects which surround us permit us to discover more and more aspects of ourselves....

> In a sense, therefore, the knowledge of a soul of things is possibly a very direct and new and revolutionary way of discovering the soul of man. The description of the power and meaning of various types of objects can bring new aspects of the personality of modern man out into the open. (1964:6)

Just as Sherlock Holmes was able to take a simple hat and, by examining it closely, learn much about the man who owned it, so we can take various objects as signs and infer a considerable amount about the culture in which the object is found and used.

I would like to take an object that I believe to be rich in meaning and an important sign, and subject it to analysis: the following are some of my hypotheses on the significance of digital watches.

Hypothesis 1.   Digital watches reflect a growth of alienation in contemporary societies. The essence of the digital method is "finger counting" which translates, when we come to machines (like clocks) to separate units. A digital watch flashes the time moment by moment, in contrast to the now "old-fashioned" analog watch which is based on relationality. We tell the time on an analog watch by looking at the position of hands on a watchface. The digital watch is atomistic; it divides time into discrete parts, which flick by rapidly. The analog watch sees time as something unified, and is rooted in history. Time passes but the cycle repeats itself every 12 hours. The atomism and separation found in the digital watch lead me to suggest that societies where such watches are popular are more alienated than those in which analog watches are most popular. It may also be that individuals who wear digital watches are more alienated than those who do not.

Hypothesis 2.   People who wear digital watches have a greater sense of powerlessness than those who wear conventional analog watches. Many of the digital watches have buttons that enable wearers to do various things (including, in some cases, calculations). Studies of the wearers of the previous generation of digital watches showed that one of the main reasons people bought digital watches was that they got a sense of power from being able to summon time, make the watch do something. This may seem incredible or even pathetic, but such seems to be the case. It seems possible that people who gain a sense of power or mastery from being able to push buttons and have a device do their bidding must suffer from a sense of powerlessness (which they might not recognize or be aware of). These watches help people with strong command imperatives and latent feelings of powerlessness deal with their problems.

Hypothesis 3.   People who wear digital watches worry more about self-control than those who wear conventional watches. Digital watches are much more precise and accurate than analog watches, which means we can be more careful about arriving on time for meetings, being where we are supposed to be when we are supposed to be there. And, God forbid, should we forget an appointment, we can set the alarm, a feature in many of the watches, so we'll be alerted. Some watches sound every hour, which suggests a great concern for and consciousness of the passage of time.

Hypothesis 4.   Digital watches enable their wearers to impose their concern about time upon others. A watch that sounds every hour makes those who hear it conscious of the passage of time, which means that individuals can exercise a certain amount of social control over others by wearing a watch with a beeper and allowing it to beep on the hour. But even if the watch doesn't beep on the hour, when others hear the beep they become concerned about what time it is. These beeping watches are a problem in concert halls which now are obliged to remind audiences to turn their watches off.

Hypothesis 5.   Digital watches reflect the triumph of the electronic over the mechanical in modern society. The traditional mechanical watches, with springs and winding mechanisms, are now old-fashioned "art objects" and do not have the power or resonance of the new electronic digital watches. Winding is a sign, generally, of the mechanical; in the electronic world one pushes buttons. There are, of course, some people who feel hostile to the new electronic order and who prize old-fashioned things like mechanical watches and other relatively crude (though often beautiful) machines. The dichotomy between mechanical and electronic watches is reflected in the following material:

Modernity	The Good Old Days
Digital Watches	Mechanical Watches
Electronic	Machines
Space-Age	Crude
Push Button	Winding

What is important about all this is that the digital watch helps us obtain a new identity, gives us a "modern" look and feeling. This space-age modern style is becoming dominant in our culture.

Hypothesis 6.   The dominance of the digital watch shows the power of fashion. Fashion is not by any means confined to clothes; fashion is a force which works on all of us and makes us want to change in some way. These changes generally involve abandoning something old for something new— whether it be hair styles, eyeglass styles, clothes, wives and husbands, or watches. Fashion works on our desire to be admired and loved, to show our ability to afford new things, or even our anxiety about being different from others. The triumph of the digital watch is an excellent example of the power of fashion to sweep people off their feet and inspire in them a passion, a need, a desire that cannot be denied. Until, of course, the digital watch is bought. As a result of the popularity of these watches, which makes it more economical to manufacture them, and of new technical developments, digital watches are now extremely inexpensive. For 10 or 15 dollars one can purchase a digital watch that is capable of doing all kinds of remarkable things. Thus one who insists on wearing a conventional watch is implicitly making a statement, is refusing to go modern. There are, of course, large numbers of people who feel this way and who pay for their prejudices, so to speak. I might add that going along with the fashions is not necessarily a sign that one is integrated in society; it may indicate, instead, anxiety stemming from alienation which leads one to try to look (at least) like everyone else.

Hypothesis 7.   Digital watches are magical toys. There is something quite remarkable about these watches—they run silently, they are very busy (with numbers appearing, in rapid succession, from nowhere—or so it seems). The watches seem to have a life of their own, a life that increasingly affects and shapes our lives. They always bubble with energy and activity while we have our periods of rest and tranquillity (or exhaustion) as well as of activity. And they do such remarkable things. In certain respects, they are adult toys. (As the saying goes, "the difference between the man and the boy is the price of the toy.") Adults relate to gadgets the way children relate to toys. Gadgets often have an aesthetic, and always have a functionality; that is, they do things and we derive a great deal of pleasure from the beauty of gadgets and their powers.

Hypothesis 8.   The digital-watch phenomenon caught the Swiss napping. The Swiss underestimated the appeal that digital watches would have and discovered, to their chagrin, that a major portion of the watch market had been "stolen" from them. This is because the Swiss watch manufacturers believed that beautiful machines would be preferred to space-age gadgets. . . an elitist conception that proved to be very costly. We now live in an electronic age and in an information society. Our love affairs with the car and other machines are just about over; we have transferred our affection to computers and other electronic devices. A magazine advertisement showed this very graphically recently. A young man says to his father, "Dad, can I borrow the computer tonight?"

In conclusion, digital watches are not simply utilitarian objects but, instead, objects with significant cultural resonance. Taken as signs, they reveal much about our values, hopes, passions, and the direction in which our society is moving.

Five

Visual Aspects of Signs

As we have seen, not all signs are visual; sounds can be signs and the same applies to smells, tastes, and textures. But many signs have a visual dimension and it is important to understand the various aspects of the visual sign which might be considered in any analysis.

1. *Use of Color.* Different colors (at least in the western world) tend to generate different emotions. Red suggests passion, danger, heat, and related emotions; blue is seen as cool and serene, ethereal. Violet is associated with royalty and richness. There is, however, no natural connection between a color and the feelings that color engenders. (This is, I might point out, a questionable position. Some disagree.) Thus, for example, in the western world we wear black when we mourn, but in other cultures white is worn.

Some might argue, for instance, that there is an obvious reason why red is used to indicate "stop" in traffic signs and signals. Red, there, stands for the blood that will be spilled if the signs are not obeyed. The question is, does the use of red always suggest danger, blood, or passion? I doubt it. Context and cultural associations are the critical factors here, not nature.

We must also be mindful, when we consider color as sign, of such matters as hue and brightness. In some instances the brightness of a color may be more important than the color itself in conveying a particular message.

2. *Size.*   When we speak of size our concern is not primarily with the dimensions of a given sign as much as with the relationship of elements within a sign or sign system. Signs vary from business cards to supergraphics that cover a whole building. In the case of supergraphics we find that a change in scale has important repercussions. Supergraphics show that words can be turned into works of art (instead of being, essentially, a means of communication). The change in scale emphasizes the asthetic components of the letters of the word rather than the word's signifying (message) function.

There is probably no place in the world where the scale of signs is of such importance as in Las Vegas. Here is Tom Wolfe describing these signs in his essay "Las Vegas (What?)" (in *The Kandy-Kolored Tangerine-Flake Streamline Baby*):

> Las Vegas is the only town in the world whose skyline is made up neither of buildings, like New York, nor of trees, like Wilbriham, Massachusetts, but signs. One can look at Las Vegas from a mile away on Route 91 and see no buildings, no trees, only signs. But such signs! They tower. They revolve, they oscillate, they soar in shapes before which the existing vocabulary of art history is helpless. I can only attempt to supply names—Boomerang Modern, Palette Curvilinear, Flash Gordon Ming-Alert Spiral, McDonald's Hamburger Parabola, Mint Casino Elliptical, Miami Beach Kidney. (1966:7)

A sixteen-story sign (especially when it soars above a two-story building) transcends its origins and becomes, in spite of itself, an *objet d'art*. It may be vulgar but it demands attention as an aesthetic statement.

3. *Spatiality.*   Here we are concerned with the relationship among elements within a sign system such as an advertisement. Some signs (such as supermarket advertisements) are very "busy" (or self-cluttered) and have relatively little display and differentiation due to a lack of "white space." Other signs, such as cosmetic advertisements in fancy magazines, are extremely simple and understated and have a great deal of "empty" space. This empty or white space is, itself, a sign—of elegance, refinement, quality.

Hall's work on proxemics has demonstrated how the spatiality of building areas affects people; the same might be said for all kinds of visual signs. As Albert Mehrabian points out in *Silent Messages*:

> The higher a person's status, the greater is the area that he can claim as his own territory and therefore the greater is the likelihood that he will retain his

You can tell from the outside which Scotch they serve on the inside.

Johnnie Walker®
Black Label Scotch
YEARS 12 OLD

12 YEAR OLD BLENDED SCOTCH WHISKY, 86.8 PROOF. BOTTLED IN SCOTLAND. IMPORTED BY SOMERSET IMPORTERS, LTD., N.Y. © 1981

Spacious grounds and huge mansions are associated with "class." Johnny Walker takes advantage of this association in its advertisement.

psychological advantage in dealing with others. So, we have a two-sided relationship. People of high status claim and regulate access to larger territories and those who already have access to large territories are able thereby to assume the advantages of high status. (1971:36)

This sense of spatiality, associated with high status in homes, buildings, and so on, also expresses itself in the spatiality found in advertisements and other visual signs.

4. *Contrast.* By contrast I mean the differences among elements in a sign in terms of such matters as color, size, shape, and texture. Contrast is used for emphasis and consists of oppositions such as light and dark, bright and dull, busy and simple, large and small. Contrast is used to "selectivize" perception, and thereby generate "display." Clutter is the enemy of contrast.

In busy signs, for example, no elements stand out. It is possible to offer a great deal of information but it is difficult to emphasize anything in particular. The same applies to streets full of competing signs. On the other hand, very simple signs cannot carry much information; their function, rather, is to generate a sensibility. The use of contrast is exemplified in traffic signals.

5. *Shape.* Shape plays an important role in generating meaning in signs. Think, for example, of the heart-shaped outline used in valentines which we have learned to associate with love. Now, red hearts meaning "love" are found in many signs, bumperstickers, and so on. In this case the meaning of the heart-shaped valentine is symbolic, not iconic. A heart does not look like a valentine. In other cases, meaning stems from the iconicity of the shape.

Thus we find Sigmund Freud in "Symbolism in Dreams" (in *A General Introduction to Psychoanalysis*) explaining phallic symbols:

> The male genital organ is symbolically represented in dreams in many different ways, with most of which the common idea underlying the comparison is easily apparent...the penis is symbolized primarily by objects which resemble it in form, being long and upstanding, such as *sticks, umbrellas, poles, trees* and the like; also by objects which, like the thing symbolized, have the property of penetrating, and consequently of injuring, the body,—that is to say pointed weapons of all sorts: *knives, daggers, lances, sabres*; fire-arms are similarly used: *guns, pistols, and revolvers*, these last being a very appropriate symbol on account of their shape. (1953:161–162)

Although Freud uses the term "symbol," he is really talking about what we would call an iconic sign.

6. *Grain.*   Grain is also a sign of some utility...or, more precisely, a symbol. It suggests—in grainy photographs, for example—amateurishness or speed (due to something like danger). If we consider "soft focus" to involve grain, then we see soft-focus images in terms of emotion, dreaminess, the imagination, and so on. Highly precise photographs, with no grain, suggest science, technology, and mechanization.

The Judy Chicago exhibit was an art show in which highly decorated plates and table settings were used to "represent" important women throughout history. I was struck by the sexual nature of the imagery used in the sculptured and "vulviform" plates.

THE JUDY CHICAGO SHOW*

The room is vast, suffused in dim light. In it stands an open, triangular table of monumental size, with 39 place settings on it. We are at "The Dinner Party," a work of art that celebrates what might be called "the feminine principle" as personified in 39 mythical and historical females who have played a major role in shaping western consciousness.

"Women have never had a Last Supper," says Judy Chicago, who organized the multimedia exhibition. "But they have had dinner parties—lots and lots of dinner parties where they facilitated conversation and nourished the people." That explains things. "The Dinner Party" is a tribute to women and an event that signifies something terribly important—a return, in women, of the sense of the sacred, especially as it applies to their bodies and their roles. "The Dinner Party" is a sacred space and it is presented as such. And just as Judy Gerowitz transformed herself into Judy Chicago, so the rather banal "dinner party" that we are all used to has been transformed into "The Dinner Party."

The idea is simply magnificent—as is the show. A dinner party for the feminine principle, a gorgeous table set for mythical and historical figures who are symbolized by the way their plates are decorated and the runners, beneath each plate, are decorated. And what is displayed on this huge table? Women glorying in their achievements and in their sexuality. The ambience of the show may be chaste but the plates are crawling with sex—vulviform shapes, labia, eggs, and Judy Chicago's personal symbol of

---

* First published as "Nourishing Art from the Rich History of Women," in *The Chronicle Review*, April 16, 1979. Reprinted with permission.

Photograph by Philip Galgiani

Virginia Woolf place setting from *The Dinner Party* © Judy Chicago 1979. Reprinted with permission.

the feminine, butterflies. "The Dinner Party" celebrates women's generativity in brilliant, festive, and assertive ways. And sexuality has become sacred. The influence of Georgia O'Keeffe, who has one of the 39 plates and is described by Chicago as "the mother of us all," is strong.

I felt somewhat like Henry Adams must have felt when he gazed upon the dynamo for the first time and recognized in it a symbol of a new order, of a new force that would transform society. Now Judy Chicago and the 200 people who spent five years working with her have presented as with something equally as compelling as the dynamo. And it isn't the Virgin, either. (She is conspicuously absent from the table, as is Eve.) It is women affirming and reveling in their sexuality, their generativity, and their creativity.

This is not to say that "The Dinner Party" does not celebrate women as artists, writers, political leaders, and mythic heroines. It most certainly does, but not at the expense of feminine sexuality.

Take the Emily Dickinson plate, for example. It is a very feminine, pink plate which combines a vulva-like center with an outer fringe of lace-like porcelain. Judy Chicago explains how she decided to present Emily Dickinson:

Whenever I thought about the Victorian lady that a woman like Dickinson was expected to be, I envisioned lace: lace collars and cuffs on her dresses, lace doilies on all the chairs, lace clothes on the tables, and lace edgings on the demure nightgowns she would wear. Imagining a female creative genius imprisoned in all that lace evolved into my concept of Dickinson's runner and plate.

So, here we have the recluse of Amherst represented as a kind of raw sexuality "imprisoned" in pink lace...a shocking conceit but somehow a fitting one.

Judy Chicago believes that art has the power to shape beliefs, to affect consciousness, and "The Dinner Party" must be seen in that light. The show is a political statement meant to change the way in which people see women and art. "I thought that if I could convey women's history through art in a way that could change people's ideas, I could make both women's experience and women's art more significant." Personally speaking, I see nothing wrong with this kind of thing. There is always the danger of people admiring art because it is "ideologically correct" rather than being beautiful, but there is no reason why a work of art cannot be beautiful and have some kind of social and political significance. Why not have the best of both worlds? And what kind of art is it that has no connection with society?

In this respect her plate for Susan B. Anthony is quite interesting. The plate is raw and vaginal, with a rather strident reddish color. The color jumps off the plate at you—which is exactly the kind of response Judy Chicago was aiming for, because she saw Anthony as a pivotal figure, a person who recognized that a transformation of fundamentals was necessary before women's rights could be respected. In "The Dinner Party" we find a Susan B. Anthony different from the one we are used to—the "Dinner Party's" Susan B. Anthony is a figure strikingly sexual, primal, genital, yet soft and smooth. The runner beneath the plate shows female figures with hatchets and liquor bottles—a different side of her personality.

I'm not sure what to call "The Dinner Party." Is it a sculpture? An exhibition? A show?

Whatever it is, it is a striking and powerful expression of femininity and, in particular, feminine sexuality. This is something that will be very difficult for many men to deal with. For thousands of years, in Western civilization, there has been a subliminal and perhaps even visceral fear of female sexuality. A father of the Church, in its early years, described women as "a temple over a sewer," reflecting the kind of fear and even loathing that many men feel towards women. This fear—perhaps even hatred, at times—has been at the root of the "woman question" for men, who suffer from drone anxieties and other bizarre afflictions.

What Judy Chicago's work offers, then, is a liberation for men at the same time that it offers support and identity for women. "The Dinner Party" is a symbol of woman's heritage and a celebration of her powers. The huge, rectangular table, presented (or is it "staged") so beautifully by The San Francisco Museum of Modern Art, is a sign that something rather dramatic has taken place. There has been a remarkable transformation in the consciousness of many women which is reflected in this exhibition. Their sense of shame in their sexuality has disappeared.

And with this has reappeared a sense of the sacredness of their roles and their sexuality. I think that everything will be different from now on. Especially our dinner parties.

Six

Problems of Signs

What follows are some of the problems we face when we deal with signs. The fact that the relationship between a signifier and signified is arbitrary, and therefore always open to question, is one problem. But there are others.

1. *Clutter.* Here the pressure from competing signs prevents a sign from having full impact. Think, for example, of some main streets in cities which are full of signs for restaurants, stores, gas stations, motels, and so on. The competition for attention leads to confusion due to information overload. We cannot absorb all the information available to us and thus block all signs out. We face the same problem with commercials and packages in supermarkets, all of which try desperately to get our attention. The signs, instead of standing out, merge into a collection or montage of signs and lose their individual identities.

2. *Code Confusion.* If there is a difference between the codes of the creators of the signs (i.e., simplicity equals elegance) and the codes of the consumers of the signs (i.e., bright colors, gaudy, busy designs equal high

class) there will be poor communication. On the most fundamental level, think about people who speak different languages. I can recall how disoriented I felt in countries such as Greece and Finland, where I had not the slightest idea of what words meant, and where, at times, I found myself trying to communicate with people who knew no English. I felt completely at a loss.

But even when people speak the same language, as a result of differences in education, class level, and cultural background, there are often problems. A given word can meant different things to different classes of people, so one must be extremely careful. Different cultures interpret a given word in different ways, also. A Japanese professor once told me that the word "pragmatic" means "tool user" in Japan, which is far removed from the way the word is understood in America.

What happens is that people from different cultures and social classes bring different codes to messages and interpret them in different ways. Umberto Eco has dealt with this phenomenon in his essay "Towards a Semiotic Inquiry Into the Television Message" (*Working Papers in Cultural Studies* 3, Autumn 1972:115):

> Codes and subcodes are applied to the message in the light of a general framework of cultural references, which constitutes the receiver's patrimony of knowledge: his ideological, ethical, religious standpoints, his psychological attitudes, his tastes, his value systems, etc.

The possibilities of aberrant decodings have always existed but whereas once aberrant decodings were the exception, they are now, Eco argues, "the rule in the mass media." (1972:106) Eco may be a bit pessimistic in his evaluation, but there can be little question that a good deal of code confusion exists, and the possibilities for its existence are enormous.

3. *Meaning Change.*   This occurs when signs become appropriated by people who use them in different ways. Once, for example, long hair was associated with musicians. Later it became a sign of "hippies" and members of the counterculture. It was taken up, then, by bikers, college professors, marginal types, and so forth. Ultimately, so many people were using long hair as a sign, for so many different reasons, that it lost its meaning and became overly diffused. That's one of the problems with signs: they can be appropriated by anyone and when this diffusion occurs, the signs lose their power to convey information reliably.

4. *Ambiguity in Signs.*   In addition to all the other problems we face in dealing with (and interpreting) signs, there is one other vexing difficulty—the fact that signs are often ambiguous. Let me suggest two cases here: one, situations in which one signifier has numerous signifieds; and two,

situations in which a number of different signifiers can suggest one signified. The cases are explained here.

One Signifier/Many Signifieds.   Think, for example, of the multiple meanings of Coca-Cola, which has been interpreted by various critics (with widely different perspectives) as suggesting such things as youth, hedonism, America, modernity, cultural imperialism, orality (Coke suckers), and so on. We can diagram this first case as follows:

$$
\begin{array}{ll}
\nearrow \text{ SFD} & \nearrow \text{ America} \\
\text{SFR} \rightarrow \text{SFD} \qquad \text{Coca-Cola} \rightarrow \text{Youth culture} \\
\searrow \text{ SFD} & \searrow \text{ Cultural imperialism} \\
& \quad\ \ \text{(Coca-colonization)}
\end{array}
$$

Many Signifiers/One Signified.   Here we might take the United States of America as our object or signified and such elements as Uncle Sam, eagles, our flag, the Washington Monument, and so on. This would be diagrammed as follows:

$$
\begin{array}{ll}
\text{SFR} \searrow & \text{Uncle Sam} \searrow \\
\text{SFR} \rightarrow \text{SFD} \qquad \text{The Flag} \rightarrow \text{U.S.A.} \\
\text{SFR} \nearrow & \text{Eagles} \nearrow
\end{array}
$$

The ambiguity found in signs gives them power, but it is also a source of confusion. Since a given sign can mean a number of different things to people or different signs can mean the same thing, we learn that we must always be circumspect when we use signs.

What was Pop Art and what did it reflect about American culture? These are two of the questions discussed in this essay on the Pop Art movement. Pop Art is seen here as a "sign" that reveals interesting things about our society.

POP GOES THE WESSELMANN

The commercialization of life in contemporary American society, which reached its zenith (or is it nadir) in the new "art form" of the television commercial, has also had an impact upon other visual arts and brought forth an interesting phenomenon—Pop Art. It made its big splash 20 years ago but is still with us. Pop Art is a form or genre that reflects the overwhelming impact of the advertising industry on the artistic consciousness. As an enthusiastic celebrant of Pop Art, S. A. Green (Curator of the Philadelphia Modern Art Museum) put it:

> Pop art's imagery is unashamedly inspired by the joys of the assembly line, and its evocation of commercial advertising reflects the mirth and joy of today's scene. The viewer is captivated by its immediacy, and the resulting participation is perfect. . . The pop artists have created a Balzacian record of our era in which cliché and banality are served up with such delectation that they inspire reverence. Size is an important feature of the new art, and repetition and magnification are standard trappings. Details may be omitted but little is left to one's imagination. (S. A. Green, in foreword to Rublowsky, 1965).

Mr. Green's assessment of American culture and the joys of the assembly line seem rather exaggerated and unrealistic but his comments are significant. They help us understand something about Pop Art and its relation to American culture.

The content of Pop Art is essentially commercial advertising and artistic techniques connected with it. This notion is not held by Green alone. In a chapter entitled "Pop Art in California" Nancy Marmer pointed out what is basic to Pop Art:

> The central novelty and perhaps most fruitful aspect of Pop Art obviously consists not in its concentration on common objects (which, after all, have appeared sporadically through art history since seventeenth-century Dutch genre painting), nor in its popular culture subjects (which provided material for earlier generations), nor in its "questioning" of the nature of the relationship between depiction and reality (all art since 1890 does that), but in its *sanction of advertising, illustration, and commercial art conventions as well as techniques for the presentation of these*, or any other figurative subjects, in a context of "high art." (Nancy Marmer, in Lippard, 1966:148)

Industry and the assembly line generate an "art form" and this "art form" and its techniques and content—advertising and commercial art—become elevated to the status of high art.

The same techniques we find in advertising—repetition and scale— become two of the specific characteristics of Pop Art which give it distinction and identity. When clichés and banal ideas and images are served up often enough, in big enough portions, and with sufficient "delectation," they ultimately inspire reverence.

Green suggests that Pop Art has a commercial character and is "an evocation of the vast spaces on our land given human personality by billboard signs." He hastens to add that this is perfectly fine:

> No apology is needed for this art or its artists. Their accomplishment stands. Theirs is an art of immediacy, of brilliance, of mirth and joy. In their work, these artists face the now, the present, the today with pleasure and acceptance. They celebrate life. Tomorrow, they leave to the future.

This "acceptance" by many Pop Artists of the present along with an unwillingness to be critical of the banality and ugliness of much that they see around them suggests there is an essential irresponsibility in the Pop Art movement (though some Pop Artists have used their work to make social commentary). In essence, if Green is correct, Pop Art is not critical or even satirical; rather, it celebrates our depersonalized and dehumanized society.

In this respect it is worth considering the various comic-strip characters and *Playboy* nudes we find in Pop Art. These subjects do not reflect a renewed interest in human personality and a humanistic perspective, but something quite different. John Rublowsky points this out:

> Abstract expressionism found its special vocabulary by turning within, by giving palpable expression to an interior vision that occurs only in the creative imagination of the artist. This is "sensibility painting" carried to its ultimate

refinement. Personal, intense, lyrical—abstract expressionism provided the perfect idiom for expressing the esthetic truth that reflected a particular moment in time.

Pop art, utilizing the same artistic freedoms, represents the opposite pole of expression. Abstract expressionism was a turning within; Pop art is a turning out. One was the ultimate in sensibility painting; the other is anti-sensibility, taking its esthetic from the brute presence of the objects it depicts. One was highly personalized; the other is depersonalized, anonymous. (Rublowsky, 1965:3, 4)

We see what Rublowsky is talking about in works such as Roy Lichtenstein's "Ice Cream Soda," Andy Warhol's "Marilyn Monroe, 1962," and Jasper John's "Painted Bronze, 1960."

There is a good deal of controversy about who is really a Pop Artist and who is (merely) derivative. Lucy Lippard, author of *Pop Art*, claims that satirists such as Marison, "Doom Artists" like Doris Lurie, common-object artists like Jim Dine and romantics like Robert Indiana are *not* Pop Artists. She admits only five "hard-core" Pop Artists to the pantheon of Pop Artistry: Andy Warhol, Roy Lichtenstein, Tom Wesselmann, James Rosenquist and Claes Oldenburg, though she suggests there are a few others of lesser stature on the West Coast and in England. It is worth noting that Pop Art is associated with New York City, which is the center of the advertising world.

Marshall McLuhan has suggested that the Pop Art movement shows that we "have begun to process the environment itself as an art form." What he doesn't mention is that we are not processing *the* environment but an aspect of the environment—the world of advertising illustrations and commercial art—which we have sanctified with the prestige of elite art. A beer can (or two) may be interesting and full of cultural resonance, but does it become a work of art if we take it from the supermarket and put it in a museum?

The popularity of Pop Art, the content of which is our commercialized environment and the "message" of which is, ultimately, the acceptance and glorification of the meretricious fantasies of Madison Avenue, is something I find most troubling. If its champions can describe Pop Art as "depersonalized" and "anonymous," what is left for its critics to say?

Seven

Denotation and Connotation

In semiological thought, denotation and connotation play stronger roles than they do in traditional linguistic study. The denoted message is the direct, specific meaning we get from a sign, and might be best explained as being, essentially, a description of a signifier. Thus, if we were concerned with an object such as a Barbie Doll, the denoted message of the Barbie Doll would be "This is a doll. It is $11\frac{1}{2}''$ tall, has measurements of $5\frac{1}{4}''-3-4\frac{1}{4}''$ and was invented in 1959." The connotative message would be quite different and would deal with the cultural baggage the doll carries—what it symbolizes, what it reflects about American culture, what effects it may be having, and so on.

Ultimately, the connotative meanings of signs turn into myths or reflect myths (and reinforce them). Thus connotation is, in many instances, an extremely powerful phenomenon. This matter is discussed in *Language and Materialism: Developments in Semiology and the Theory of the Subject*, by Rosalind Coward and John Ellis:

> The mechanism of myth is the way that habitual representations tangle themselves up in everyday objects and practices so that these ideological

meanings come to seem natural, the common-sense reality of that object or practice. There are therefore two systems of meaning: the denotative and the connotative, the "object-language" (the film, the toy, the meal, the car, inasmuch as they signify), and the myth which attaches itself to it, which takes advantage of the form of this denotative language to insinuate itself. (1977:28)

Part of the semiological enterprise, then, becomes disentangling the myth (or "mythology" as Barthes would put it) from the denotated sign.

In *Mythologies* Barthes offers us an example:

I am at the barber's, and a copy of *Paris-Match* is offered to me. On the cover, a young Negro in a French uniform is saluting, with his eyes uplifted, probably fixed on a fold of the tricolor. All this is the meaning of the picture. But, whether naively or not, I see very well what it signifies to me: that France is a great empire, that all her sons, without any color discrimination, faithfully serve under her flag, and that there is no better answer to the detractors of an alleged colonialism than the zeal shown by this Negro in serving his so-called oppressor. (1972:116)

A historical situation—France's colonialism and militarism—is now made to seem natural, something to be taken for granted, something to be dismissed without thought. (Here I am using "dismissed" as "accepted" and "not worth even thinking about since it is part of that which goes without saying.")

Technically speaking, myth, for Barthes, is a second-order semiological system in which signs in the first-order system (the combination of signifiers and signifieds) become "a mere signifier in the second" (1972:114). In other words, the sign in a linguistic system becomes a signifier in a mythic system and the unity of the signifier and signified in the mythic system Barthes calls "signification." Barthes uses special language to distinguish the mythic system from language per se, and describes the signifier in myth as form and the signified in myth as concept. The combination of the two, as I mentioned, is the signification.

The following chart helps make all this clearer:

Language	*Myth*
Signifier	Form
Signified	Concept
Sign	Signification

What happens is that signifier and signified form the sign on the language plane and this sign becomes a signifier for a different signified and sign on the myth plane. When we are dealing with myth, the signifier (which was the sign on the language plane) is called a form, the signified a concept, and the resultant sign, a signification.

We see that the entire sign, in the denotative system, functions as the signifier in the connotative system or mythic system. The task of the analyst of signs, then, is to show how denotation and connotation work together to make signs intelligible to people. Which means, above all, to explain their signification—and this involves eliciting the concepts that Barthes describes as important "constituting elements" of myth. As he writes, (1972: 120–121) "If I want to decipher myths, I must somehow be able to name concepts." To do so he is forced, at times, to invent neologisms such as *Sininess* (for "Chinese-ness"). This is necessary because the dictionary is often inadequate.

For many years comic strips were seen merely as "junk": subliterary art forms...mostly for children. In recent years however, scholars have recognized that comics are a valuable means of understanding our culture and much serious work has been done on them. In this essay, some of our more important comic strips are discussed in terms of the values they reflect and the kind of heroes and heroines they offer to the American public.

FUNNY WHAT YOU CAN FIND IN THE FUNNIES*

1. ***Remembrance of Comics Past.***   I can remember the appeal comics had for me when I was growing up. The colors in the Sunday editions, which seem so crude now, had a raw power and luminous intensity that thrilled me. I can recall, in particular, the gorgeous purple of The Phantom's costume. What did I know, then, about racism and fascism, which a number of commentators have found in the strip? To me there was something mysterious and wondrous about him as he moved, silently and regally, through his jungle kingdom. (When we are young and innocent comics have a reality and fascination that is hard to explain or describe.)

Weekdays there was Dick Tracy and his bestiary of grotesques—Pruneface, Flattop, The Mole, Shoulders, Flyface, and so on, lethal and sinister killers who generally ended their days with a slug from Tracy through their heads. The strip had an ambience of violence and terror permeating it, created, in part, by Gould's dramatic use of black and white. In those days "Li'l Abner" was still going strong and Capp, still a liberal, peopled his strip with remarkable and fantastic comic creations

---

* A modified form of this essay, "Taking Comics Seriously," appeared in *The Wilson Quarterly*, Summer 1978. Reprinted with permission of *The Wilson Quarterly*.

such as Shmoos, and Kigmies, and characters like Joe Btfsplk, Marryin' Sam, and Fatback J. Roaringham.

"Joe Palooka," "The Gumps," "Terry and the Pirates"—these strips and others contributed to a vast and fascinating American pop mythology which has only recently been "discovered" by scholars in America and which is yielding inestimable riches to our social historians and critics. We seldom think about it but many of our strips have been appearing for 50 or even 60 years. "Mutt and Jeff" started in 1907, "The Captain and the Kids" appeared in 1914, "Blondie" in 1930, and "Dick Tracy" in 1931.

Even "Peanuts," a relative newcomer, dates back to 1950. In the more than 30 years of its existence, Schulz (who does everything himself) has drawn something like 10,000 episodes of "Peanuts" and, assuming an average of four or five panels per episode, has worked on between 40,000 and 50,000 panels. He has had to think up a gag every day for more than 30 years, and the same applies to all the other artists who create humorous strips.

The other kind of comics—serial or narrative adventure strips—pose other problems, namely the matter of maintaining continuity and reader interest in a continuing story for 30 or 40 years. With the rise of television, many daily adventure strips have become casualties, in part because they cannot compete with television in generating entertainment excitement but also because the syndicates have not been enterprising in developing new talent. In any case, the comic strip (an art form that involves continuing characters, pictorial narration, and dialogue or language carried within the picture frame) is still flourishing and still chronicles our society as it has since the turn of the century.

Comics are an American idiom. They reached their greatest popularity and development here and reflect both our genius and our spirit. Because of this American comics are studied assiduously now as "cultural indicators" which reveal much about our values and beliefs, and many other things, often hidden from our awareness.

2.   *The Kid is Father to the Man (Super, Bat, Plastic, etc.).*   There is a considerable amount of disagreement about when the prototype of the comic strip appeared. Some say it was Cleopatra's Needles, other Trajan's columns and still others the Bayeux Tapestry. Maurice Horn, in *The World Encyclopedia of Comics*, suggests that none of the above are correct and locates the first "strivings" toward the comics in Leonardo Da Vinci's *Notebooks*, though it was Hogarth, he says, who finally assembled "the two heterogenous elements of text and image into a single whole." (1976:9) Other artists who deserve mention are Wilhelm Busch, creator of "Max and Moritz," and George Colomb or "Christophe" who made some interesting stylistic innovations. Both pushed the comic strip toward its modern form.

As far as American comics are concerned, however, there is general agreement that "The Yellow Kid," which made its appearance on May 5, 1895, was our first comic strip. "The Yellow Kid" became extremely popular and according to Stephen Becker, author of *Comic Art in America*, evoked "that first, gentle wave of mass hysteria which accompanies the birth of popular art forms. The Yellow Kid was soon on buttons, cracker tins, cigarette packs and ladies' fans; eventually he became a character in a Broadway play."(1959:10) The "commercialization" of "Peanuts" and other comic strips is, we find, nothing new.

The hero of "The Yellow Kid" strip, a strange-looking, bald, jug-eared youth, who generally wears a nightshirt, inhabits a squalid slum, Hogan's Alley. It is packed with numerous other children who, however, are decidedly not childish. They often wear derbies, smoke cigars and cigarettes, and sometimes are even bearded. The panels in the strip are often exceedingly busy, crowded with humans, animals, signs, posters and other objects. There are numerous comments about political figures and social concerns written on walls or the Kid's nightshirt.

There is something rather poignant and heroic about the Kid and his friends who inhabit Hogan's Alley. They seem abandoned—by parents too busy or tired to look after them—and are the first of a long line of "abandoned" figures we find in the comics. This sense of abandonment is connected, I believe, to our historical experience of having left the old world, our "fatherland," for a new world of hope and opportunity. Our attempt to "escape from history" has cost us a great deal, in psychological terms, as the "Roots" phenomenon suggests. We have become what I call "spiritual orphans."

One thing our examination of "The Yellow Kid" reveals is that the most important messages we find in comics are seldom consciously placed in them by their creators. Thus the spatiality of "The Yellow Kid" and its use of grotesques is more revealing than allusions in the strip to social and political matters.

Some strips such as "Li'l Abner," "Pogo," "Dick Tracy," and "Little Orphan Annie" have rather obvious social and political implications but this does not mean we cannot find other kinds of important information in them and in other strips and books which, at first sight, seem innocuous and trivial. One reason the comics are so useful to the analyst is that they are so innocent and so devoid of self-consciousness. In the comics we do not find the "rehearsed response."

3. *What the Comics Tell Us.* Comics can be analyzed much the same way other artistic and literary creations are—in terms of the symbolic significance of their heroes and heroines and villains, their narrative structure, the art work and language, the values and attitudes reflected, the psychodynamics of their characters, and so on. A comic strip is, after all, a

series of images and images are resonant, or, as Ezra Pound wrote, an image is "that which presents an intellectual and emotional complex in an instant of time." (Quoted in Tindall, 1955:103) In the case of comics, the images are graphic and usually accompanied by language so that we are actually presented with a formidable and complex aesthetic problem in trying to interpret and explicate comics.

We can see this when we examine what is probably our greatest comic strip, "Krazy Kat." Herriman's use of semiabstract, shifting backgrounds and his remarkable rhetoric show the possibilities within the art form. There is even an existential dimension to the strip which, for 35 years, featured a willful, anarchistic mouse named Ignatz throwing bricks at a love-sick Krazy Kat, who took the bricks as signs of love. She, in turn, is loved by Offissa Pupp, who tries desperately to protect Krazy from Ignatz's bricks and locks him up in prison time after time, to no avail.

Listen to one of Herriman's characters rhapsodizing on work:

> Indolence—the sin of the century...the error of the era—And labor is so lovely...toil so transcendent...the witchery of work so wondrous...industry looks upon the world with beauty...Diligence is a dainty delight...Endeavor is an enchanting endowment...Effort effuses an affluent afflorescent effulgence...it is noble to strive, brave to strain, kingly to struggle...

An examination of "Krazy Kat" shows that it reflects two important themes: the triumph of illusion over reality (Krazy's ideas about the bricks) and the victory of rebelliousness over authority (Ignatz's refusal to stop throwing bricks, though he is punished for it repeatedly). Both of these themes reflect important components of the American psyche and character.

In some strips the political content or ideology, so submerged in "Krazy Kat", appears rather overtly. "Little Orphan Annie" is a case in point. This little waif spent something like 40 years (starting in 1924) railing against the direction American society was taking and championing the old, homely, conservative, small-town values of our earlier years. She is an important symbolic figure in our comic pantheon because she is one of our most significant "spiritual orphans" (along with Superman, Batman, Plastic Man, Spider Man, and so on), and it is her mission to lead us forward by returning us to the old-fashioned verities. Ultimately she ends up as an apologist for corporate capitalism. Here is an extract from the August 31, 1945 strip:

> *Annie*: But *why* did some papers and commentators say such terrible things?

> *Warbucks*: Oh, I guess it was fashionable to sneer at "big incomes." They fail to mention that most of those big incomes go to pay everyone's bills and make the load lighter for everyone else. I believe that the more a man makes honestly, the more he helps this country and everybody in it. What I think we need is a lot more million-a-year men! Mighty little *they* can *keep* anyway...

She never convinced many people but she did provide millions of people with excellent entertainment.

With "Doonesbury," our most important new comic strip, the political content is so direct and obvious that the line between comics and political cartoons almost disappears. Trudeau is a brilliant political and social satirist who won the Pulitzer Prize in 1975 for his work. He satirizes a number of contemporary figures and types in the strip and since his allusions are so immediate, he is a very good guide to the social scene in contemporary America. We also find satire in many of the underground comics, but they are infinitely less genial and polite than "Doonesbury." They contain savage and often heavy-handed attacks upon so-called bourgeois American culture.

They are also, at times, lively and brilliantly executed, using pornography and anything else they can think of as a means of "defamiliarizing" Americans and shocking them out of their supposedly complacent ways and blindness. The names of many of these comics reveal their satirical and subversive intent: "Subvert Comics," "Greaster (Stories to Dull the Imagination)" "Big Ass Comics," "Despair Comics," "Inner City Romance," "Biochemical Warfare Funnies," "Zap" and "Young Lust," to name just some of them.

There is, ironically, a difference between the stances found in many of these comics and their supposedly "liberated" point of view. Robert Crumb, creator of one of the leading underground heroes, Mr. Natural, fills his work with admittedly "hostile and often brutal acts against women" but he argues, in a proclamation (in comic-strip format) "And Now a Word To You Feminist Women" that as an artist he should be free to do whatever he wishes. He writes:

> Well, listen you dumb-assed broads. I'm gonna draw what I fucking-well please to draw, and if you don't like it, FUCK YOU!

Mr. Natural is a hip capitalist guru who has no compunctions about fleecing gullible people of their money and bedding down with any woman he can find. The underground comics may not believe in romantic love, but in fighting against it they often end up with a rather unhealthy point of view in which sexuality becomes depersonalized and debased.

Much of what we find in comics, as this brief discussion of sexuality suggests, demands a psychoanalytic approach if we are to understand things fully. For example, in the underground comics, sex degenerates to a kind of comic and nonrelational satisfaction of biological urges which is close to the Puritanical view of sex as obligatory (and dangerous).

And what about Dick Tracy's awesome, single-minded, almost pathological preoccupation with evil (and our fascination with him)? He is a superego figure who helps us deal with problems of guilt we all feel, and his ritualistic combats with grotesque characters allow us the luxury of guilt-free aggression in the name of justice.

Some people have suggested that there is something perverse in the relationship between Batman and his ward Robin. There is also the matter of Dagwood Bumpstead's orally fixated eating jags which can be seen as a means he uses to compensate for his powerlessness and impotence. "Blondie" is the most popular comic strip in America and reveals a great deal about the American family and male–female relations despite its seeming innocuousness and absurdity. Few readers know that Dagwood was once a man-about-town and playboy figure. He became domesticated terribly quickly, it seems, and his haircut, with its "cuckold" locks, symbolizes the depths to which he has sunk.

When you look at these "collective daydreams" carefully you see that they contain is a remarkable amount of compulsive, somewhat neurotic behavior. Many characters are humorous and made ridiculous, but even so, beneath the humor there are troublesome personality characteristics and neurotic syndromes that cannot be ignored.

The most successful innovation in comics, which saved the comic-book industry, was the development of multidimensional, humanized, and often disturbed characters such as Spider Man. At the end of one of his adventures, in a state of amnesia, he laments:

I'm someone called Spider Man! Someone with no yesterdays—and with no tomorrow.

There is something terribly sad about this. Not only is he speaking for himself but he also echoes, I fear, a sense of futility felt by many of the young people who follow his adventures so avidly.

4. *Taking Comics Seriously.* The "funnies" (an inaccurate word) have been with us for some 80 years, during which time we have generally regarded them as trivial entertainments for children (and adults who wish for happy moments of regression). Journalists have had great sport with academics who "read meaning" into the comics and the creators of many comic strips have vehemently denied that they were up to anything significant, or that their work was worth bothering with. We are constantly told that comics (or films or television programs) should be enjoyed and not analyzed—because there is nothing in them to analyze.

I reject this "know-nothingism" as naive and ill-founded. I hope this brief essay will help convince you that comics are an important and significant means toward understanding American character and culture. Like slips of the tongue and dreams, which Freud has suggested reveal our most secret souls, the comics have much to tell us, if we will only ask.

Eight

Imaginary Signs

Imaginary signs are signs that don't exist in the real world but, rather, in our mind's eye. I include under imaginary signs all forms of signs that are visual but which are generated by our minds. I also include here descriptions of things in addition to the more conventional category of imagined phenomena such as visions and dreams.

1. *Verbal Descriptions.* Here words are used to "paint a picture" which the reader sees in his or her mind. An example from Dostoyevsky's *Crime and Punishment* follows:

> He was a man over fifty, bald and grizzled, of medium height, and stoutly built. His face, bloated from continual drinking, was of a yellow, even greenish tinge, with swollen eyelids out of which keen reddish eyes gleamed like little chinks. (1945:12)

Each reader will see this person in a different way, but it is obvious that the written word has considerable power as far as creating pictures of an imaginary nature are concerned. In this brief passage we have a number of descriptive terms: *bald, grizzled, stout, bloated, yellow, greenish, swollen, keen, reddish*. Taken together they help generate a highly defined image of the character being described.

2. **Dreams.**   Dreams can be defined, for our purposes, as imaginary signs that we generate during sleep. How dreams are created and the ways they function are quite complicated. Recent research has shown that dreams are exceedingly important to us and not just something accidental and trivial. Freud believes that dreams are essentially images. In *The Interpretation of Dreams* he writes:

> Now dreams think essentially in images; and with the approach of sleep, it is possible to observe how, in different proportion as voluntary activities become more difficult, involuntary ideas arise, all of which fall into the class of images...Dreams construct a *situation* out of these images. (1965:82–83)

All of us, since we all dream, are "creative" then, though our creations may puzzle and confuse us.

One reason for this confusion is that in our dreams we manipulate images—we substitute one image for another or put bits and pieces of different images together—in an effort to evade the censorship of our superegos. Also, our dreams are always connected, so Freud argued, to our experiences, so a symbol in one dream doesn't have precisely the same meaning as a symbol in another dream (or the same symbol is someone else's dream). Certain symbols, as I pointed out earlier, because of their shape, for example, do have a general meaning, however—phallic symbols and related phenomena.

Dreams play an important role in *The Bible*. Think, for example, of Joseph's dreams and what these dreams reflected about his relationship with his brothers:

> ...for behold, we were binding sheaves in the field, and, lo, my sheaf arose, and also stood upright; and, behold, your sheaves stood round about, and made obeisance to my sheaf. (Gen. 37:7)

and:

> ...behold, the sun and the moon and the eleven stars made obeisance to me. (Gen. 37:9)

These dreams caused his brothers to envy him and conspire against him, and cast him in a pit. It was also Joseph's ability to interpret dreams— that is, to understand the significance of dreams, to give them what we might call a semiological reading—which led to his becoming ruler over Egypt for the Pharaoh.

3. *Hallucinations.*   Hallucinations are defined as perceptions of objects that are not real, and that are caused by various forms of disorders of the nervous system. Some typical examples might be hallucinations of oases that thirsty travelers in the deserts "see," or hallucinations generated by drugs. Psychologists distinguish between delusions, which are false beliefs, and hallucinations, which are sensations or imagined perceptions of things not present.

In *Psychopathology and Society*, Nathan and Harris discuss the phenomenon:

> A *hallucination* is the perception of a sensory stimulus which does not in fact exist. The patient may see something which is not there, hear something when no sound has been made, or smell, taste, or touch something for which there is no external stimulus.... The most common hallucinations of the schizophrenic are auditory...the patient hears voices talking to him or about him. They may command him to do certain things, or they may call him names and make fun of him. The voices may be those of God, the Devil, the patient's mother, or strangers.... Although visual hallucinations are less common than auditory ones, they are not uncommon among people diagnosed as schizophrenic. The patient may have religious visions, or see frightening or amusing scenes. (1975:160)

The authors point out that hallucinations are had by people other than schizophrenics. Some people in the counterculture (and in other subcultures) seek hallucinatory experiences and ingest various hallucinogens to obtain these experiences. They equate some form of "higher wisdom" with such experiences, though there is considerable doubt, among scientists, that this alleged "higher wisdom" or "transcendent consciousness" is, in fact, superior to ordinary consciousness (or even equal to it).

4. *Visions.*   Visions usually have a supernatural or revelatory nature. They are "ways of knowing" but they are very problematical, since one person's vision is another person's hallucination. *Webster's Ninth New Collegiate Dictionary* defines vision as follows:

> something seen in a dream, trance, or ecstasy; *specif*: a supernatural appearance that conveys a revelation.*

Visionaries are defined as people who are dreamy, see things that are illusory, are impractical and utopian.

The problem with visions is that some of them seem to be of great

---

* By permission. From Webster's Ninth New Collegiate Dictionary © 1983 by Merriam-Webster, Inc., Publishers of the Merriam-Webster® Dictionaries.

consequence, so we cannot dismiss them the way we dismiss hallucinations. Visions are not associated with psychotic states but, generally, with religious states (though there are some who would equate the two). To further complicate matters, visions are often difficult to interpret and understand. We often feel that there may be something important in a vision, but we feel frustrated in not being able to fathom the meaning of the vision.

Take the vision of the prophet Ezekiel, a portion of which follows:

> Now it came to pass...as I was among the captives by the river Chebar, that the heavens were opened, and I saw visions of God...And I looked, and, behold, a whirlwind came out of the north, a great cloud, and a fire infolding itself, and a brightness was about it, and out of the midst thereof as the colour of amber, out of the midst of the fire. Also out of the midst thereof came the likeness of four living creatures. And this was their appearance; they had the likeness of a man. And every one had four faces, and every one had four wings. And their feet were straight feet; and the sole of their feet was like the sole of a calf's foot; and they sparkled like the colour of burnished brass. And they had the hands of a man under their wings on their four sides; and they four had their faces and their wings. Their wings were joined one to another; they turned not when they went; they went every one straight forward. As for the likeness of their faces, they four had the face of a man, and the face of a lion, on the right side: and they four had the face of an ox on the left side; they four also had the face of an eagle. Thus were their faces.... (Ezek. 1:1–11)

> Now as I beheld the living creatures, behold one wheel upon the earth by the living creatures, with his four faces. The appearance of the wheels and their work was like unto the colour of a beryl: and they four had one likeness: and their appearance and their work was as it were a wheel in the middle of a wheel. When they went, they went upon their four sides: and they turned not when they went. As for their rings, they were so high that they were dreadful; and their rings were full of eyes round about them four. And when the living creatures went, the wheels went by them: and when the living creatures were lifted up from earth, the wheels were lifted up.... (Ezek. 1:15–19)

What sense do we make of all this? Was Ezekiel a madman and is this vision nothing but the ravings of a psychotic? Or is there something important buried in the arcane symbolism? Is this, in fact, a vision, per se—an imagined sight—or is it, as Ezekiel suggests, a description of something he actually saw.

Notice, for example, that he is very precise in his descriptions. I did not quote the material in which he tells when he saw the vision, but he is very specific on the matter:

> Now it came to pass in the thirtieth year, in the fourth month, in the fifth day of the month...(Ezek. 1:1)

and later:

In the fifth day of the month, which was the fifth year of King Jehoiachin's captivity.... (Ezek. 1:2)

So he is well oriented and tells us when he had the vision, not once but twice. This may be a technique to establish credibility, but if so, it indicates rationality and a mind in control of itself.

It may be that Ezekiel was perfectly conscious and "made up" his vision; after all, his mission was to preach to the Jews and help them follow the commandments of their creator. Thus, it could be that his visions were elaborately contrived fictions which had a pragmatic and very specific function. If so, this vision—and all the other wondrous events described in the book of Ezekiel—show a mind of extraordinary creative ability. This interpretation would suggest that Ezekiel wasn't a madman but, instead, a literary genius.

There is another interpretation which argues that what Ezekiel described in the passage quoted earlier was an Unidentified Flying Object (UFO) and its crew of aliens or extraterrestrials. The mysterious wheels Ezekiel talks about are his way of characterizing a space ship, which touched down in his presence. Thus what we find in Ezekiel is not a vision full of his own fantasies, but, instead, a description of something fantastic in itself. This interpretation is, of course, speculative and far-fetched. And that is one of the main problems we face when we deal with visions. They are fantastic and generate fantastic intepretations.

We all dream, and at some point we all speculate about the meaning of a dream we have had. In this application I use Sigmund Freud's theories to explicate the hidden meaning of a dream of one of his patients. The techniques that Freud elaborated can be used to understand other phenomena involving "visual imagery," such as magazine advertisements, commercials, television programs, and so on.

FREUD ON DREAMS

Freud is one of those remarkable thinkers whose works have been read by few, damned by many, and used—as they have filtered into the public consciousness—by almost everyone. What most people know about Freud is that he believed in infantile sexuality, that he saw phallic symbols everywhere, that he believed in all kinds of crazy things like the Oedipus Complex, penis envy in women, castration anxiety in men, and so on. One reads, constantly, of Freud's having said "sometimes a cigar is only a cigar" (which implies, if you think about it, that sometimes a cigar isn't only a cigar) and he is constantly castigated for having asked "What do women want?"

Freud, for many people, is seen as a "radical" thinker who had some wild ideas that have generally been repudiated. On the other hand, much of Freud's conceptual apparatus has been adopted by the general public and it is not unusual to read articles on such matters as rationalization, the id, ego and superego, anxiety, and so on.

A huge number of books are published every year which apply, adapt, modify, or reject Freudian concepts, and increasingly large numbers of people are seeing therapists of every persuasion. One way or another it seems to be Freud with whom we must be reckon. One problem is that there are many Freuds. Because his thought evolved over the course of his long and distinguished career, it is difficult to be certain what Freud really thought. In addition, each critic or celebrant of Freud creates his or her own Freud, so the matter becomes further complicated. One is always on risky ground when talking about Freud.

I hope to avoid the problems I've just discussed by concentrating on a rather brief portion of one of Freud's essays, "The Occurrence in Dreams of Material from Fairy-Tales" written in 1913. Those who are unfamiliar with the details of Freud's notions about sexuality and symbolization will find it a bit extreme, perhaps. And those who are not sympathetic with Freudian concepts will probably find the analysis far-fetched. But I offer it as a good example of Freudian thinking. The essay was written a number of years after Freud's masterpiece, *The Interpretation of Dreams*, which explains, in great detail, his theories about how dreams function and how they should be interpreted.

There are several points Freud makes in *The Interpretation of Dreams* which will help us with his fairy-tale essay. First, dreams involve wish fulfillments. Second, dreams often involve distortions and disguises. Third, two of the most important forms of distortion are condensation and displacement. Condensation involves "the construction of collective and composite figures," in which one figure is used to represent many different figures or bits and pieces from a number of different images are combined into one. Displacement involves the substitution of one image or element in a dream for something else, generally this involves the substitution of something seemingly innocuous (and asexual) for something that might alert the "dream-censor" and cause us to wake up. Third, we often dream about matters indirectly connected to our activities and thoughts of the previous days. Finally, there is a process called "secondary elaboration" in which we take the images in the dream and turn them into a coherent story.

With these notions in mind, let us consider a dream Freud analyzes in "The Occurrence in Dreams of Material from Fairy-Tales." It is a dream by a young married woman who had been visited by her husband a few days before she had the dream.

> She was in a room that was entirely brown. A little door led to the top of a steep staircase, and up this staircase there came into the room a curious manikin—small, with white hair, a bald top to his head and a red nose. He danced round the room in front of her, carried on in the funniest way, and then went down the staircase again. He was dressed in a grey garment, through which his whole figure was visible. (A correction was made subsequently: He was wearing a long black coat and grey trousers.) (1963:59–60)

RENÉ MAGRITTE: *La Clé des songes*. Collection privée.

RENÉ MAGRITTE: *Le Vent et le Chant*. Collection privée.

Signs may be used to lie. Here Magritte is obviously misleading us, but in some cases we are not aware we are being lied to.

In order to simplify and clarify Freud's analysis of this dream, I will list the points he makes.

The Manikin.   *His personal appearance was that of the dreamer's father-in-law.* Freud adds, "Immediately afterwards, however, the story of 'Rumpelstiltskin' occurred to her, for he danced around in the same funny way as the man in the dream and in so doing betrayed his name to the queen." As a result of this, Freud adds, Rumpelstiltskin lost his claim upon the Queen's first child and became so furious with himself that he tore himself in two. It turns out that the woman who had the dream had been so angry with her husband that she had exclaimed, "I could tear him in two."

The Brown Room.   *The dining room of the woman's parents was brown.* The woman then told stories about beds that were uncomfortable for two people to sleep in and recounted that she had been with a group of people and said something "mal à propos" that led everyone to roar with laughter. Symbolically the brown dining room represented a bed and ultimately, through its connection with food, a double bed. The visitor was not her husband but her father-in-law.

This interpretation leads Freud on to a more profound, deeper analysis of the dream which focuses upon its sexual content. He writes:

> The room, at this level, was the vagina. (The room was in her—this was reversed in the dream.) The little man who made grimaces and behaved so funnily was the penis. The narrow door and the steep stairs confirmed the view that the situation was a representation of coitus. (1963:61)

The woman was able to interpret the grey garment (which was transparent) as a condom. This was connected to her anxiety about getting pregnant after having had sexual relations with her husband.

The Black Coat.   *The woman liked to see her husband dressed nicely instead of the way he usually dressed.* The black coat refers to an image of her husband that the woman liked. When he was dressed in a black coat and the grey trousers she was getting, in a sense, the best of both worlds.

Freud suggests that there is an interesting reversal going on in this dream. The little man has come not to take the Queen's child away but, instead, to bring a second child. Freud concludes his analysis of the dream as follows:

> ...Rumpelstiltskin also gave access to the deeper, infantile stratum of the dream-thoughts. The droll little fellow, whose very name is unknown, whose secret is so eagerly canvassed, who can perform such extraordinary tricks—in the fairy-tale he turns straw into gold—the fury against him, or rather against

his possesor, who is envied for possessing him (the penis-envy felt by girls)—all these are elements whose relation to the foundations of the patient's neurosis can, as I have said, barely be touched upon in this paper. The short-cut hair of the manikin was no doubt also connected with the subject of castration.

If we carefully observe from clear instances the way in which the dreamer uses the fairy-tale and the point at which he brings it in, we may perhaps also succeed in picking up some hints which will help in interpreting any remaining obscurities in the fairy-tale itself. (1963:61–62)

Dreams are always connected to the lives of the people who dream them and the signs and symbols found in dreams can only be interpreted individually, in terms of the history of the person having the dream. Freud argued that there is *no* codex that explains the meaning of signs and symbols without regard to the dreamer's experiences. Dreams can be interpreted and function as a royal road to the unconscious of the dreamer (and the repressed wishes of the dreamer, as well). But dreams—and we dream in disconnected images, he believes—are always and only meaningful in terms of the individuals who have them.

It is possible, I believe, to take Freud's model and apply it to cultures. If we substitute mass-mediated dreams (films, television programs, commercials, novels, comic books) for the individual dream, and matters such as national character, culture, and society for the individual dreamer, we find ourselves with interesting possibilities.

Dreams, Freud tells us, are functional; they have a meaning and they do something for the dreamer. In the same light, our collective dreams (or is it daydreams) have a meaning and provide people with a number of gratifications. What are they and why are they important? When we look upon our popular culture, or mass-mediated culture, as being like dreams, employing the same condensations and distortions (and other tricks), we find ourselves with material that is not trivial but, instead, rich with possibilities for analysis and understanding.

Nine

Signs that Lie

It has already been suggested that if signs can tell the truth, they can also lie. The power that a sign has to communicate "true" information can also be used to communicate "false" information. I've already quoted Umberto Eco who argues, in his *A Theory of Semiotics*, that "semiotics is in principle that discipline studying everything which can be used in order to lie." (1976:7)

Much human behavior is based on this fact; it is what makes life so interesting and people-watching so fascinating. For we must always wonder when we are being misled, why we are being lied to, and how it is done. In the list that follows I will briefly describe some of the more common examples of signs that lie—taken from a wide variety of different fields. In certain situations (poker, for example) we expect to be lied to; in others, we anticipate "white lies." Sometimes we even lie or mislead people with signs and symbols without any sense that we are doing wrong (using status symbols that are "above" us). But there are many other cases as described in the following list when we are genuinely duped.

Area	*Misleading Signs*
Transvestite	Clothes of opposite sex
Wigs	Different hair color, style
Dyed hair	Different hair color and "personality"
Impersonation	Appropriation of identity in general
Imposter	Appropriation of profession
Parody	Appropriation of literary style, genre
Camouflage	Blending into environment
Falsies	Big breasts
Accents	Fake nationalities
Malingering	Unreal illness
Pseudointellectual	Jargon, clothes, and so on
Mock turtle soup	Calf's head with reptilian pretensions
Passing	Appropriation of a different race
Theatre	Pretended feelings, beliefs, and so on

It should be obvious that we must spend a great deal of time and effort trying to figure out when we are being "conned." Blondes turn out to be brunettes, voluptuous women turn out to be flat, husky men turn out to be shrimps when they take off their padded jackets and elevator shoes, surgeons turn out to be college drop-outs, and that breakfast of sausages and scrambled eggs you had this morning turns out to have been made of soybeans.

Because our lives are so full of pretense and pretending, a number of sociologists have taken the theatre as the basic metaphor for understanding social relations. From this perspective we are all actors and actresses playing roles with others, who are also actors and actresses. If you take this as a given, you can understand—in a more profound sense—why many people act the way they do.

There are obvious reasons why people "lie" with signs—they get certain payoffs that they consider worthwhile. Thus, in a society where "gentlemen prefer blondes" and where blondes are symbols of sexiness, it pays to be a blonde. That's why blonde hair dye is the most popular color sold. But blondeness, like all signs, has a number of different meanings, many of which are not evident to the women who blonde their hair. As Charles Winick points out in *The New People*, many women blonde their hair to escape their ethnic background or to cover gray hair.

But there are other, more interesting aspects to blonding:

> ...for a substantial number of women, the attraction of blondeness is less an opportunity to have more fun than the communication of a withdrawal of emotion, a lack of passion. One reason for Marilyn Monroe's enormous popularity was that she was less a tempestuous temptress than a nonthreaten-

ing child. The innocence conveyed by blonde hair is also suggested by the 70 percent of baby dolls whose hair is blonde.

> D. H. Lawrence pointed out that blonde women in American novels are often cool and unobtainable, while the dark women represent passion. Fictional blondes also tend to be vindictive and frigid. (1968:169)

Thus we face the ironic situation in which a woman dyes her hair blonde thinking she is communicating one thing while, really, she is communicating something else. Here she is using a false sign (her blondeness) to lie but, unintentionally, in a communication from her unconscious, she is telling the truth (about her sexuality).

The matter is a complicated one, since men, who allegedly see blondes as "sexy" on the surface, must also have an understanding of their real nature—an understanding they may not be conscious of, I might add. There is also the matter of atavistic attitudes involving light and darkness, equated with good and evil, which are at play here. Light hair becomes symbolic of goodness, innocence, and so on. The work of psychiatrist Roderick Gorney is relevant here. In a review of his book, *The Human Agenda, Newsweek* magazine focuses attention on his discussion of "The Quest for Blondeness":

> ...he attempts to demonstrate a parallel between white man's worshipful attitude toward blondes and his racial fear and hatred of blacks. Do blondes really have more fun? "She is likely to find that she is expected not so much to *have* more fun as to *be* more fun, particularly by men who want to exploit her for their own real, although more covert, adventures in regression to the Fun ethic of childhood," Gorney writes. "A man will want her to have the 'innocent sweetness' of childhood combined with a mature genital sexuality of which no child is capable." He thinks building a "self" based on this blond image partly explains the tragedy of Marilyn Monroe. (12 June 1972:100)

Gorney's analysis meshes with that of Winick; both see the blonde as innocent and connected with childhood and sweetness and not with mature sexuality and passion. Men would be attracted to these "innocent" women because they would not be experienced and thus less judgmental about men's sexual performances—if, that is, things were ever to get to that stage. Gentlemen may prefer blondes, then, for a wide variety of reasons (the most important of which, however, deal with anxiety about sexual ability).

Let me say a few words about imposters now. I made a distinction in my list between impersonators, who take on a particular person's identity, and imposters, who appropriate a profession. Obviously there are cases in which an imposter impersonates someone so he or she can gain credibility and the requisite certifications in order—ultimately—to obtain a particular position: surgeon, teacher, and so on. We can understand the payoffs imposters get by considering the career of the "great imposter" Ferdinand Waldo Demara, as it was described in his obituary (*San Francisco Chronicle*, 9 June 1982).

Demara was described by a friend of his, Melvin Belli (a famous San Francisco attorney) as "a man who was bitten by an imp.... He had no great corporations to run, no prisons to direct, no operations to perform, so he invented it."

The obituary goes on to describe some of Demara's triumphs:

> In his assumed identities, Demara lived as a Trappist monk, a doctor of psychology, a dean of the school of philosophy at a small college in Pennsylvania, a law student, a zoology graduate, a career researcher, a teacher at a junior college in Maine, a surgeon in the Royal Canadian Navy, an assistant warden at a Texas prison and a teacher in a Maine village.

His secret, according to another friend, was in being able to "read and retain technical books. He could learn it all in three to six months." What Demara did in all his roles was to learn the jargon associated with the role—or, to use the semiological perspective, to appropriate the signifiers. When one added the false certifications he obtained, it is quite plausible that he would succeed—if only briefly. Imposters succeed because we tend to give people the benefit of the doubt; if they are credentialed, know the correct lingo, and act the right way, we assume they are who and what they say they are.

Despite what must have been formidable acting talents, Demara was always anxious. His physician, Dr. John J. Zane of Anaheim was quoted in the obituary as saying that "Demara was never happy in any of his deceptions and always lived in fear of being discovered." It is conceivable that this tension the imposter feels has positive as well as negative aspects, and gives a person a heightened sense of drama about his or her life. Demara turned out to be a rather tragic figure, according to the obituary. He died alone and in obscurity, "the most miserable, unhappy man I have known," said his doctor.

In most cases, the use of false signs is relatively trivial and of little moment; we use false signs because they "pay off" and are worth the bother. There are situations, however, as the Demara case suggests, in which the matter is more serious.

Berger after Capp.

The fact that signs can be used to "lie" as well as tell the truth gives them both power and complexity. From the semiological perspective, parody relies on the fact that we recognize that someone is, in a sense, lying . . .or pretending, to be more specific. We must know what is being parodied to enjoy fully the humor in parody.

ON PARODY

Parodies are humorous and satirical imitations of famous works of literature, of authors with distinctive styles, of certain forms or genres of writing and, ultimately, of anything (or anyone) with a strong identity. Parodies give us pleasure only when we are familiar with the work or writer being imitated. The purpose of parody is to amuse people, to make them laugh.

I classify parody as a *technique* of humor (as contrasted to a *form* of humor, such as the joke or riddle) which uses, in turn, other techniques of humor such as wordplay, exaggeration, and facetiousness, to name just a few. Humor is one of the most enigmatic subjects—one that has attracted the attention of the greatest philosophers and thinkers for thousands of years. They have generally been concerned with why people laugh . . .and despite a great deal of effort, nobody seems to have been able to answer the question to the satisfaction of many others. My interest in humor has taken a slightly different tack; instead of wondering *why* we laugh I have investigated *what* makes us laugh. I have elicited some 45 different techniques found in all humor which, in turn, can be classified under four general kinds of humor: Humor of Language, Humor of Logic, Humor of Identity, and Humor of Action. These techniques are listed in the chart that follows.

Basic Techniques of Humor

Language	Logic	Identity	Action
Allusion	Absurdity	Before/After	Chase Scenes
Bombast	Accident	Burlesque	Slapstick
Definition	Analogy	Caricature	Speed
Exaggeration	Catalogue	Embarassment	
Facetiousness	Coincidence	Eccentricity	
Insults	Comparison	Exposure	
Infantilism	Disappointment	Grotesque	
Irony	Ignorance	Imitation	
Misunderstanding	Mistakes	Impersonation	
Over-Literalness	Repetition	Mimicry	
Puns and Wordplay	Reversal	Parody	
Repartee	Rigidity	Scale	
Ridicule	Theme &	Stereotype	
Sarcasm	Variation	Unmasking	
Satire			

These techniques give us an anatomy of humor and are found in humor of all sorts, in all genres, in all forms. An understanding of these techniques allows us to see how humor is generated, to determine what makes us laugh (even if we don't understand why it is that we do laugh). The "Why" theories give us interesting ideas about humor in general but aren't helpful when it comes down to individual cases. Some of the more important theories of why we laugh are as follows:

Hobbes   Laughter is based on superiority.
Freud   Laughter is based on masked aggression.
Bergson   Humor involves the mechanical imposed on the living.

Each of these theories might help us understand something like parody, but they are all at such a high level of generalization that they don't help us with specific works of parody.

Hobbes wrote, in *The Leviathan*, "The passion of laughter is nothing else but sudden glory arising from a sudden conception of some eminency in ourselves by comparison with the infirmity of others, or with our own formerly." Perhaps we find parody amusing because we feel superior to the writer being parodied and enjoy the appropriation of his identity for purposes of ridicule. In *Jokes and Their Relation to The Unconscious*, Freud discusses parody and related techniques:

Caricature, parody and travesty (as well as their practical counterpart, unmasking) are directed against people and objects which lay claim to authority and respect, which are in some sense *"sublime."* They are procedures for *Herabstzung* (degradation).... (1963:200)

He explains how all this works as follows:

Parody and *travesty* achieve the degradation of something exalted...by destroying the unity that exists between people's characters as we know them and their speeches and actions, by replacing either the exalted figures or their utterances by inferior ones. (1963:201)

From Freud's perspective the aggressive content of parody is quite strong and it really represents a rather powerful attack on artistic (and other forms of) identity.

For Bergson, who wrote that humor is "something mechanical encrusted on the living," we must assume that the parody is a "mechanical" rendering of something originally distinctive and "live." Like Freud, Bergson has something to say about parody. He first established a general rule, *"A comic effect is always obtainable by transposing the natural expression of an idea into another key."* (Quoted in Sypher, ed. 1956:140).

Bergson then discusses parody:

Transpose the solemn into the familiar and the result in parody. The effect of parody, thus defined, extends to instances in which the idea expressed in familiar terms is one that, if only in deference to custom, ought to be pitched in another key. (Sypher 1956:140–141).

Bergson mentions degradation theories of parody but argues that what is crucial in parody is not degradation but transposition and, in fact, that degradation is only one form of transposition.

These theories are interesting and give us some fascinating insights into the nature of parody but they are also rather abstract and general. Perhaps, at this stage, it would be best to look at a parody and see what we find in it. Here is a brief selection from Woody Allen's "Spring Bulletin," a marvelous parody of college catalogue course descriptions.

Introduction to Psychology: The theory of human behavior. Why some men are called "lovely individuals" and why there are others you just want to pinch. Is there a split between mind and body, and, if so, which is better to have? Aggression and rebellion are discussed. (Students particularly interested in these aspects of psychology are advised to take one of these Winter Term courses: Introduction to Hostility; Intermediate Hostility; Advanced Hatred; Theoretical Foundations of Loathing.) Special consideration is given to a study of consciousness as opposed to unconsciousness, with many helpful hints on how to remain conscious.

Philosophy I: Everyone from Plato to Camus is read and the following topics are covered:
Ethics: The categorial imperative and six ways to make it work for you.
Aesthetics: Is art the mirror of life, or what?
Metaphysics: What happens to the soul after death? How does it manage?
Epistemology: Is knowledge knowable? If not, how do we know this?
The Absurd: Why existence is often considered silly, particularly for men who wear brown-and-white shoes. Manyness and oneness are studied as they relate to otherness. (Students achieving oneness will move ahead to twoness.) (1967: 38)

"Spring Bulletin" is quite obviously a parody of a highly defined genre, but it is more than that. It is also a devastating satire on both psychology and philosophy courses and their "subjects"—at least as they are taught in many colleges and universities. Allen uses absurdity to spoof the "logic" of these disciplines. Given the alleged "split" between mind and body, which is better to have? Can we know? And if we can't, how do we know this? The questions are, in truth, interesting questions; but in the context of the essay they seem quite ridiculous. Allen also makes good use of a form of incongruity I describe as "defeated expectations" and "disappointment." We see this in passages in which he starts out seriously and then turns silly or sarcastic. Thus, after he mentions the "categorical imperative" of Kant he spoofs the self-help phenomenon by adding "and six ways to make it work for you."

His use of language is particularly interesting. He wonders why existence is often considered "silly" and has a good deal of fun playing around with "manyness," "oneness" and "twoness." In the same manner, he takes off on the concept of "aggression" with his mad sequence of courses: "Introduction to Hostility; Intermediate Hostility; Advanced Hatred; Theoretical Foundations of Loathing." Here we have the form of the traditional description of courses and sequences of courses, but the content is sheer nonsense.

From this discussion I hope it will be evident that parody is a humorous technique that makes use of other techniques leading to works that implicitly make a comment on what is being parodied and also provide wonderful entertainment.

Ten

Men's Looks: Signifiers and Life-Style

There's a wonderful cartoon which shows two politicians talking. One says to the other, "My image was designed by...." and then he names some company. "Who designed you?" he asks.

The point of this is that we consciously use signs to present an image to others—an image that we believe others will interpret in very specific ways. Since the relationship between a signifier and signified is arbitrary, it is convention—and read here "advertising, the mass media, and so on"— which tells people what to associate with what. In certain cases function is also important: mountaineering boots imply climbing or hiking and the type of person we associate with this activity.

Because signs can be used to lie, it is always possible to find people manipulating these signs. In fact, manipulation may be what creating an "image" is all about. In the chart that follows I will list some of the signs men use to create an impression, image, and identity, and I'll suggest what each sign "means" to people. I will consider such matters as hair style, clothes, props, shoes, glasses, and ties.

In some of the explanations of "signifieds" that follow I will be arbitrary and even frivolous in order best to express the meaning of the signs.

Signifiers and Perceived Life-Styles

Signifier	Signified
Long hair	Counterculture (especially if dirty)
Short hair	Businessman (square)
Very short hair	Gay or military or both
Crew cut	Military
Tan	Sports-loving, leisure class
Pale	Intellectual (therefore sickly also)
Levi's	Casual, proletarian?
Designer jeans	Classy, wealthy
K-Mart jeans	Working class
Three-piece pin stripe	Executive, businessman
Briefcase	Old-fashioned
Attaché case	Conventional business type
Hand purse	Europhile, pseudo-Italian
Day pack	Outdoorsy
Shopping bag	Peasant
Sandals	Arty
Wingtips	Business type
Work boots	Laborer
Hiking boots	Environmentalist, hiker
Aviator glasses	Middle-class square
Wires	Antiquarian
Dark sunglasses	Gangster type, paranoid
Bow tie	Egghead
Thick tie	Behind the times
String tie	Hick, westerner

There are just a small sampling of the signs men use to present themselves to others. I've not said anything about facial hair, jewelry, belts, shirtstyles, and so forth.

Nor have I said anything about signs in subcultures, such as the use of keys, handkerchiefs, web-cotton belts, and lumberjack shirts among certain homosexual groups in San Francisco, or leather among sadomasochist groups. Probably the most obvious example of the use of signs to reflect an image (and more than that, a philosophy, politics, etc.) can be seen in the punk phenomenon. Punks dyed their hair strange colors and cut it in bizarre ways, they wore unusual clothes, used props (safety pins stuck through their nostrils, for example) to attract attention and convey their message.

Photograph by Jan Browman

San Francisco punk.

Bernice Martin, in *A Sociology of Contemporary Cultural Change*, discusses the origin of the punk movement in England; it surfaced around 1975–1976 and was declared "dead" there a year later:

It seems to have begun life in a few obscure London clubs with a largely working-class clientele, and in its beginnings it may have been an authentic backlash of the lumpenproletariat re-creating simple beat music that needed no special skills, and spitting out both the general alienation of the unemployed and the *machismo* and chauvinistic attitudes native to many lower-working-class milieux (after all, we are only one brief generation on from the skinheads). The middle classes invaded it very early, scenting a new, raw, non-commercial, underdog authenticity here. (1981:176, 177)

The middle-class elements made it more sophisticated and modified it considerably:

> Just as it did in the sixties, the take-over of the bohemian middle class turns lumpen crudities into sophisticated subtlety. Simple if violent taboo breaking gives way to camp double-takers and all the usual apparatus of anarchic anti-structure derived from the avant-garde arts, vaudeville and the rest. Surrealism, Dada, and pop art are easily detected as directed influences on dress, self-presentation, lyrics, and music. (1981:177)

Thus punk's expressive content is derived from elite art forms and used by middle-class types, for the most part (especially in America) for a variety of purposes. Ultimately, according to Martin, the punk phenomenon loses its identity. Its use of signs becomes ambiguous and punk ends up being "all things to all classes." What we have here, if Martin is correct, is something analogous to literary irony, in which something means its opposite. Thus, the use of fascist insignia by English punks was not an expression of a sympathy with this political philosophy but just the opposite—a "put on," so to speak...a means of attracting attention and provoking "square" middle-class people.

In American society, punks seem to be drawn from middle-class elements, who do not find themselves in the same situation that working-class youth do in Great Britain. The punk movement in America seems to involve personal, sexual, stylistic matters rather than political matters, and punk here seems a fad for those who like to experiment with their identities.

The fact that middle-class types in England and America have taken over punk shows how difficult it is to be certain that one's interpretation of a sign is correct. Signs change their meaning, are appropriated by different people all the time; so, interpreting signs is always a risky matter.

Punks are an example of what Orrin E. Klapp calls "style rebels." In his *Collective Search for Identity* he discusses the beliefs of these style rebels:

> ...the fight to modify oneself arbitrarily in any way that one pleases; denial of obligation to stick to styles appropriate to one's class or station; the fight to pose more or less deceptively as something else than what one is; the right to have kicks in any way that one pleases; the right to shock other people by being noisy, obstreperous, bad-mannered, uncouth, and obscene in public; the right to maintain a style in private life which has no relation to the style of one's occupation (as the right of a judge to be a playboy in after hours). The enlargement of the concept of identity came from the psychoanalytic revolution of the twentieth century—and from the existentialist concept of realizing oneself by rebelling. I call this enlarged concept of the right to identity the new romanticism. (1969:87)

He lists five different modes of style rebellion: mockery, dandyism, negligence, barbarism, and puritanism. It seems obvious that punks would fit into his barbarism category best, though there are also other modes involved here.

What is crucial to remember here is that all of this image building or style rebellion is done through signs. The power of people to "read" signs is what is important, though we must not neglect the ability people have to misread signs, as well—or be led astray by signs that lie.

What do blue jeans "mean" to people? How does one explain the world-wide popularity of these clothes? How does one make sense of the passion people seem to have for denims? I offer a theory—that we are experiencing what I call "denimization" and that our blue-jeans craze is functional in various ways.

DENIMIZATION*

Let us take a person who is dressed as any one of millions of people might be dressed. He is wearing cotton underpants, a cotton tee-shirt, a blue denim work shirt, a pair of Levi's, cotton stockings, and a pair of Levi's shoes. (This person, incidentally, could be a she if a couple of changes are made.) What we have here is what I call "denimization," a fashion style that has been sweeping the western world recently.

What does denimization mean? How does one explain it? In order to do this, following the analogy of language (which suggests that meaning stems from relationships and, in particular, oppositions), we must contrast denim with its polar opposite, high fashion. Denim, for our purposes, and certainly in its original manifestation, was low fashion and has been identified as "work" clothing. It was cheap and strong—two virtues that were Levi's main selling points. Garments found in high fashion, on the other hand, are generally made of fancy fabrics and cost much more money.

Fashionable clothes have been traditionally associated with leisure, and certainly not with physical work; executives or playboys don't (or

* Previously published in JOPER (*Journal of Physical Education and Recreation*), (October 1978), 23. Reprinted with permission.

didn't before the great revolution) wear denims, while truckdrivers do. Also, high-fashion clothes imply individuality and discrimination as contrasted with the mass-produced and uniform-like denims. When one buys clothing, he or she never gets completely individualized garments, unless they are tailor-made—and even these garments usually conform to certain stylistic guidelines. Thus, there is a world of difference between a suit or dress made at a fancy tailor's shop and a pair of denim pants picked up in a department store.

There are other polarities which reflect denim's cultural message:

Denim—High-Fashion Polarity

High Fashion	Low Fashion
Fancy Material	Denim (common material)
Leisure	Work
Individuality	Uniformity
Personal	Mass-produced
Boutique	Factory

A glance at this chart, which shows what denim means (or used to mean) in relation to "fancy" clothes, shows that something has happened to denim. There has been a great transformation and denim now has different meanings from those it used to have. For, curiously enough, anything that can be said for fancy clothes or haute couture can now be said of denim—it is often used in high fashion, it is often associated with leisure and play, it is often personalized and purchased at boutiques, which means it is no longer always cheap. And, with the development of all the new synthetic fibers and the scarcity of cotton, denim has become a relatively "fancy" material.

There are several interesting morals to be drawn from all this. In the first place, denim's "rise" in the world is very much part of the so-called American Dream, which says that anyone can rise in the world if he has enough willpower and a bit of luck. Denim is one more immigrant—de Nimes (from Nimes, France)—which has made good in America.

Also, denimization symbolizes, I believe, a significant change taking place in American society, in which work is losing its identity and transforming itself, more and more, into play. It is not too much of an exaggeration to say that work, often, is becoming more like play and vice versa. This can be seen clearly if you examine the relationship between fashion and work. In many areas people wear what would formerly have been defined as "play" garments to work and, at the same time, we have the phenomenon of "leisure suits."

The change in the clothes we wear is an indicator of changes in our attitudes toward work and play. Transformations (or perhaps radical dislocations) in these attitudes are evident all around us. Recently I had an opportunity to meet an editor at a local newspaper. I was dressed casually and when I was introduced to him at his office he looked at me with an expression of shocked incredulity. "You...you don't look like a professor," he said. "In my day professors looked like professors." In many universities, denimization has made such a great impact that the professors look like the janitors—and quite often the janitors look like professors. Many doctors now have abandoned their white coats and may appear in a consulting room in sandals and sport shirts. The same applies to people in many other areas.

If I am right, then, work and play have lost their separate identities and are no longer polar opposites. This has generated changes in our fashions, in which denim has become a kind of universally acceptable garment system, which does not serve the purpose of differentiating but rather of masking and of unifying. Denim is ecumenical and universalistic and, as such, mystifies by deidentifying its wearers. It is a perfect mode of disguise, and most people know it.

Some people have seen denimization as an indication of leveling downward and egalitarianism, but this view is questionable. It can be argued that it is more correct to see it as a movement away from conspicuous consumption by the rich and an aping of the rich by the middle classes. In an interview, Patrick Moynihan commented that the students at Harvard, where he once taught, "dressed poor," which can be translated into denimization and other similar manifestations. Whether this was an assertion of their rejection of "bourgeois" society (and identification with the working classes) or an effort to disguise themselves and play the game of "guess what class I'm from" is hard to determine. Personally I would assume the latter is the case, and that denimization reflects an attempt to escape from one's family and class history more often than not.

Whatever the case, denimization and "dressing poor" can cost a great deal of money nowadays—but that is a matter to be taken up at some other time.

Eleven

Coherence in Signs

Our discussion of signs to this point has focused on the individual sign, but it is obvious that signs tend to "hang together" in systems or patterns. Signs tend to coexist with other similar signs much the way upper-class people tend to associate with other upper-class people. This coherence in signs leads me to offer the following speculations.

In some cases where we have a large number of signs but one or two signs are missing (for one reason or another) we can generally fill in the missing signs without fear of going too far astray. I would call this *sign closure.* If we consider a playboy, for example, to be a sign system, we know what kinds of cars, after-shave lotions, or sweaters he probably would be wearing or purchasing, even if he doesn't have these items. One becomes a playboy by manipulating signs, which are connected to certain attitudes and expectations one develops about members of the opposite sex, just as one becomes a "punk" by using signs. The sign system I've been discussing might also be called "style" or "image."

On the other hand, if we know we are dealing with a playboy and have only one or two signs of "playboyness," so to speak, we can easily construct the image and select the proper signs to generate the proper image. I call this *sign construction*. Actually, this is probably what happens most of the time. Someone decides to become a playboy and then, as the result of reading *Playboy*, observing playboys, and so on, constructs a playboy identity by manipulating signs that others will interpret correctly—especially playgirls.

Of course, there is a problem here. One may see a man with some signs one interprets as "playboy" and assume—incorrectly—that the person is or wants to be thought of as a playboy. That may not be true at all. Thus, we run into the problem of stereotyping. We take one aspect of some individual, who is usually a member of some group we have an image of, for example, Scots, and we assume we know other things about the individual (such as that he's "cheap" or has a wry sense of humor) from that one aspect (Scottishness). It would seem that either *sign closure* (I know about Scots and he's a Scot, therefore he must be cheap) or *sign construction* (he's wearing a kilt so he must be a Scot and I know about Scots) or perhaps even both processes work in stereotyping. Sociologists have pointed out that stereotypes can be positive, negative, or mixed, and maintain themselves by selective perception, selective interpretation, selective identification, and selective exception. But these processes still keep stereotypes alive and justify them; therefore, to the extent that stereotyping is destructive, these processes have negative consequences.

It is important to remember that although there is coherence to be found in systems, there is also variety. A person may be a playboy for instance, but there are all kinds of playboys, too.

A high percentage of works in the public arts and formulaic—with relatively conventional character types, plots and settings. Here we consider the nature of formulas and whether formulaic works of art must be, by definition, poor.

FORMULAS IN THE PUBLIC ARTS

The notion that there are systems of signs—collections of signs that are coherent, related, and fit together logically—is very helpful in understanding genres in the arts, both popular and elite. The media carry genres or *kinds* of programs, books, and so on. The dominant media are television, radio, newspapers, magazines, records, and films. I could extend the list considerably. Each of these media can carry a variety of different public art forms such as news, commercials (or print advertising), situation comedies, sports programs, police adventures, soap operas, game shows, reviews (of films, television programs, restaurants), documentaries, spy stories, and so on.

It has been suggested that the major difference between the "elite" arts and the public arts is that the former are characterized by invention and the latter by convention. As John Cawelti writes in *The Six-Gun Mystique*:

> All cultural products contain a mixture of two elements: conventions and inventions. Conventions are elements which are known to both the creator and his audience beforehand—they consist of things like favorite plots, stereotyped characters, accepted ideas, commonly known metaphors and other linguistic devices, etc. Inventions, on the other hand, are elements which are uniquely imagined by the creator such as new kinds of characters, ideas, or linguistic forms. (1971:27)

Cawelti cites Joyce's *Finnegan's Wake* as a work which is at one extreme end of the invention–convention continuum and the formulaic works in the public arts at the other extreme, though he argues that many works contain elements of both invention and convention.

He defines a formula as "a conventional system for structuring cultural products," and it is the word system that is crucial for our purposes. (1971:29) There is a kind of coherence to formulas; they fit together logically and make sense. There are a number of reasons why the public arts are so formulaic. First, the writers are under pressure to create enormous amounts of material. These writers do not have the luxury of taking a year or two to produce a story; in television, for instance, successful series demand a new story every week. In such situations it is easier to fool around with a formula than think up something original.

In addition, the audiences of the mass media know the essential formulas and thus are able to understand, quickly and easily, what is going on in the stories they see and read. As a rule, the wider the desired audience, the more formulaic the product must be. A formula is analogous

Formulaic Elements in Public Art Forms

Art Form/Genre	Classic Western	Science Fiction	Hard-Boiled Detective	Family Sitcom
Time	1800s	Future	Present	Anytime
Location	Edge of civilization	Space	City	Suburbs
Protagonist	Cowboy (Lone Indiv.)	Astronaut	Detective	Father (Figure)
Heroine	Schoolmarm	Spacegal	Damsel in distress	Mother (Figure)
Villain	Outlaws Killers	Aliens	Killer	Boss Neighbor
Secondary Characters	Townsfolk Indians	Technicians in Spacecraft	Cops Underworld	Kids Dogs
Plot	Restore law and order	Repel aliens	Find killer	Solve problem
Theme	Justice	Triumph of humanity	Pursuit and discovery	Chaos and confusion
Costume	Cowboy hat, boots, etc.	High-tech uniforms	Raincoat	Regular clothes
Locomotion	Horse	Spaceship	Beat-up car	Station wagon
Weaponry	Sixgun Rifle	Rayguns	Pistol Fists	Insults

to a cliché; what you say may not be original but people will not have too much trouble understanding you. And that is important in the public arts, especially in television, where one frequently doesn't have much time to establish character or develop motivation.

In the chart on page 86 I list some of the more important aspects of formulas and apply them to some of the major art forms or genres (I am using the two words, form and genre, to mean the same thing).

This chart, I must point out, represents a great simplification; there are a considerable number of different kinds of westerns, science-fiction adventures, detective stories, and situation comedies. What I have done is suggest some of the more common elements in some of the more common formulas. The chart should be looked upon as offering, essentially, a point of departure for discussions of formulas in the public arts.

I might add that just because something is formulaic doesn't mean it isn't or can't be good. Conversely, just because something is antiformulaic or nonformulaic and highly inventive doesn't mean it must be good. There are many great science-fiction novels, detective novels, television situation comedies, and other formulaic works and equally many second-rate novels and collections of poetry. In the final analysis, it isn't so much the art form or the formula that matters, but the artist(s).

The debates about popular culture (whether it "must" cater to the so-called "lowest common denominator" and therefore be "subliterary") are generally carried out high up on the ladder of abstraction. If, instead of arguing about what "must" be the case, we look at the works themselves, we will be much better off. Somewhere between the two extremes of masterpieces created by artistic geniuses and schlock works created by hacks, there is considerable room for maneuvering by talented creators who can use and adapt formulas to generate works of value and interest.

Humorists have had great fun with the most extreme aspects of the public arts, the "schlock" material one finds in romance novels, western songs, and so on. What follows on page 88 is the formula (and its various possibilities) for the romance novel, taken from *The Wilson Quarterly*, Summer 1978.

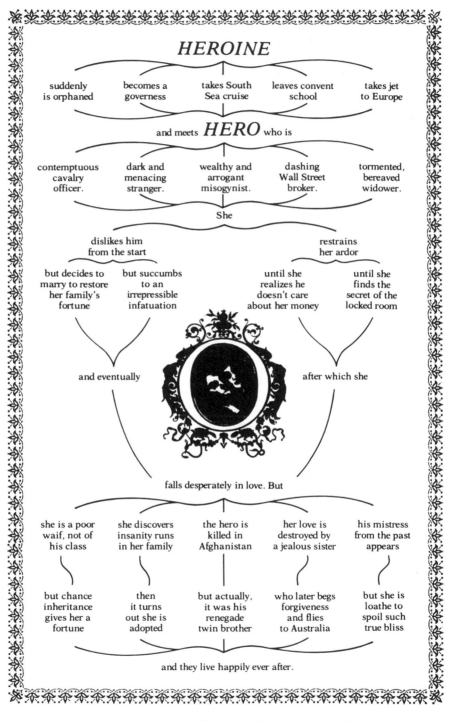

HEROINE

| suddenly is orphaned | becomes a governess | takes South Sea cruise | leaves convent school | takes jet to Europe |

and meets *HERO* who is

| contemptuous cavalry officer. | dark and menacing stranger. | wealthy and arrogant misogynist. | dashing Wall Street broker. | tormented, bereaved widower. |

She

| dislikes him from the start | | | restrains her ardor |

| but decides to marry to restore her family's fortune | but succumbs to an irrepressible infatuation | | until she realizes he doesn't care about her money | until she finds the secret of the locked room |

and eventually   after which she

falls desperately in love. But

| she is a poor waif, not of his class | she discovers insanity runs in her family | the hero is killed in Afghanistan | her love is destroyed by a jealous sister | his mistress from the past appears |

| but chance inheritance gives her a fortune | then it turns out she is adopted | but actually, it was his renegade twin brother | who later begs forgiveness and flies to Australia | but she is loathe to spoil such true bliss |

and they live happily ever after.

Formula for Romance Novel. Reprinted with permission of *The Wilson Quarterly*.

Twelve

Who Uses Signs?

If, as Peirce argued, the universe is "perfused" with signs (if not made up entirely of them), it pays to take a look at some of the people who use signs and the ways in which they use them. I will do this by offering a chart in which I list some of the various occupations or professions in which "the sign" is used, the signifiers which these people are concerned with, and the signifieds involved.

Area	Signifier	Signified
Medicine	Symptom	Illness
Military	Insignia	Rank
Theatre	Facial expression	Emotional state
Design	Form	Ethos
Detection	Clue	Criminality
Anthropology	Artifact	Cultural stage
Romance	Diamond	Eternal love
Sociology	Rolls Royce	Status

Reprinted with permission of *The Wilson Quarterly*.

This is just a sampling of a huge field. In *A Theory of Semiotics*, Umberto Eco offers a list of some of the "boundaries of the field" such as: zoosemiotics, olfactory signs, tactile communication, codes of taste, paralinguistics, medical semiotics, kinesics and proxemics, musical codes, formalized languages, written languages, natural languages, visual communication, systems of objects, plot structure, aesthetic texts, mass communications, rhetoric, etc. (1976:9–10) In the final analysis, all communication among humans is open to semiological analysis. As Eco puts it, *"every act of communication to or between human beings ... presupposes a signification system as its necessary condition."* (1976:9)

Let's take medicine as an example. The diagnostic process in medicine involves tracing symptoms and signs to diseases.* At times a patient may have many symptoms, but only some of them are important. The relation between the symptom and the disease is an indexical one and the diagnostician must be able to trace symptoms and diseases that do not, at first glance, seem to be related. To do this, the doctor must have a profound understanding of the human body and how it functions. What complicates matters is the fact that a given disease may have a number of different symptoms or a given symptom may indicate a number of different ailments. It is the ambiguity of signs that makes them so problematical...and makes diagnosis an art.

This use of signs in medicine, incidentally, is not confined to physical ailments; psychiatrists also are concerned with signifiers such as blocks, obsessions, compulsions, etc., and use, as one of their chief therapeutic instruments, an important form of signs—words. The signifiers for psychiatrists are words, behaviors, and actions, which are used to indicate various mental ailments.

Consider, for example, the definition of a hebephrenic schizophrenic offered in Hinsie and Campbell's *Psychiatric Dictionary* (Fourth Edition):

> A chronic form of schizophrenia characterized by marked disorders in thinking, incoherence, severe emotional disturbance, wild excitement alternating with tearfulness and depression, vivid hallucinations, and absurd, bizarre delusions which are prolific, fleeting, and frequently concerned with ideas of omnipotence, sex change, cosmic identity, and rebirth (the so-called phylogenetic symptoms). (1970:682)

Because of the complexities involved, it is often difficult to diagnose a given patient properly, and psychiatrists often disagree in their assessments of a person's behavior as a signifier of a specific mental illness. Thus there was a battle of psychiatrists concerning whether John Hinckley was insane

---

* Symptoms are subjective and are told to the physician by the patient. Signs are objective and are observed by the physician.

or sane when he shot President Reagan. Defense psychiatrists interpreted his behavior as indicative of insanity and thus supported the insanity plea of Hinckley's defense lawyers. But psychiatrists testifying in behalf of the prosecution argued that Hinckley was not insane at the time of the shooting and that the insanity plea was unjustified. When experts in arcane matters disagree, great problems are raised for lay people who have to make decisions.

I might point out, in passing here, that lawyers are very conscious of nonverbal behavior and other semiological considerations in selecting jury members; much work has been done on how to choose winning juries.

There are many other areas that could be investigated here, but one seems particularly important, and that is the area of design. I'm interested in such matters as the design of chairs, office machinery, kitchen appliances, and so on. There is a trend in design toward making such objects much more streamlined than they were in the past, and contemporary design of such objects might be characterized by terms such as "high tech," pseudofunctional (as in "form follows function"), simple, stark and understated.

These objects clearly reflect a fascination—if not intoxication—with science (if not scientism), technology, and elite, avant-garde aesthetic sensibilities. Thus, some modern, plastic, designer chairs, which cost a great deal of money, are beautiful to look at but terribly uncomfortable. In other words, in some cases, these objects *look* functional but aren't. They are used as signifiers of a sophisticated sensibility, of elevated taste, and of affluence—though they may also indicate sterility and lack of individuality. "High Tech" may mean "modern" to some and "trendy" to others.

POETRY AS SIGN

People don't read much poetry nowadays, but when we were younger, and in school, most of us were exposed to a bit of it. (We tend to get our poetry now in a somewhat bastardized form—in radio and television commercials as well as in songs, but we do not think of ads or songs as "poetry.")

One important sign of poetry is visual. Poems are typeset in a rather distinctive way, with each line of the poem usually being given its own identity. In other words, when we look at a poem in a book we can generally recognize it as a poem by the fact that it is set in lines and there's a good deal of white space around it.

Let me show this by printing a poem as it might appear in prose format and then printing it in its traditional poetic format, in which the spatiality of the printing serves as a sign indicating "this is a poem." The poem is a comic one called "The Frisbee": *I asked Neptune's sun, Pluto—why did you put Mercury on Uranus? He did not answer me.*

Now let me show you how the poem looks when printed as poetry:

The Frisbee

I asked
Neptune's Sun
Pluto—

Why did you put
Mercury
On Uranus??

He did not
Answer me.

A.A.B.

Without so much as reading a word of it, the reader recognizes this as a poem. The typography serves as sign here. But there are other signs in poems, in addition to the shape of the typography. There can also be a rhyme scheme. "The Frisbee" is not rhymed and so seems less a poem (in the conventional sense) than it would were it rhymed.

Here is a poem that rhymes; now we have two signs which reinforce one another and give the work more of a poetic identity.

The Paradox of the Universe

I like to think of trinities,
And all kinds of divinities
But I can only add to Two
So there is little left to do...
Except content myself with schisms
And other kinds of dualisms.

My life of length and width
Is quite conventional
But I forever am in ecstasy
In anticipation of
The third dimensional.

A.A.B.

"The Paradox of the Universe" is obviously a poem because of the way it is set in type and because it has a rhyme scheme. But it lacks something we usually associate with poetry, especially if we only have a casual under-standing of poetry, namely *meter*. Poems not only rhyme but they should (so we believe) have a regular structure.

Another sign of poetry (for the common man, and for the common woman, too) involves what might be called "poetic language." I am thinking here of words such as "thee" (as in "How do I love thee") and "thou," which come from poetry written several hundred years ago, when "real" poetry was written. I'm also thinking of the use of metaphors and similes, as we find in this selection from *Isaiah*:

> The voice said "Cry."
> And he said, "What shall I cry?"
> "All flesh is grass,
> And all the goodliness thereof is as the flower of the field:
> The grass withereth, the flower fadeth:
> Because the spirit of the Lord bloweth upon it:
> Surely the people is grass."
>
> (Isaiah 40:6)

This is highly poetic language with metaphors, similes, and archaic language, all of which signify "poem" to the reader.

Poems also derive identity from their authors and place of publication. If a so-called poet writes something, we have good reason to assume it will be a poem—at least for the conventionally minded person. If what these poets write is published in a magazine or book where we might expect to find poetry, that makes the case even stronger. Finally, if the typography is that which we associate with poetry and if there is a meter and rhyme scheme, we have additional clues.

Actually, much poetry violates all or many of the conventions just described. I've been discussing the way the average person, with little familiarity of poetry, sees poetry and understands it. For the most part poetry is a sign system, one which attracts little interest, except in its commercialized forms and formats.

"Poetry makes nothing happen," wrote W. H. Auden, one of the great contemporary poets. He wasn't listening to the radio, obviously. Or he didn't think that the advertising jingles and song lyrics were poetry. Advertising jingles may not be good poems but they do make things happen, which stems from the fact that they function both as poems and as signs—in the most literal, commercial sense of the term. The poets who work for advertising agencies are just about the only people making a living from poetry. That's a sign, too—or perhaps it is closer to being a symptom.

Thirteen

Signs and Identity

We have seen that a wide variety of people are involved with signs and signification in everything from medicine to theatre. In this chapter, I will consider the way signs are used by people to give others identity clues. I will deal with the following aspects of identity here: personal identity, national identity, occupational identity, corporate identity, gender identity, and religious identity. By identity I mean the state of being "the same as others" in certain respects and maintaining a certain coherence in style.

In *The Collective Search for Identity*, Orrin Klapp points out that identity is not a function of material possessions per se, but, instead, is connected to symbolic phenomena, and the way one is perceived by others. He writes:

> Strictly it includes all things a person may legitimately and reliably say about himself—his status, his name, his personality, his past life. But if his social context is unreliable, it follows that he cannot say anything legitimately and reliably about himself. His statements of identity have no more reliability than a currency which depends upon the willingness of people to recognize it and accept it. (1969:5)

Others must interpret one's signs of identity correctly for a person's identity to be understood and validated. In the chart that follows I list some common identity signs we use to establish various aspects of our identity.

Identity Area	Sign
Personal	Clothes
	Hair style
	Kind of glasses
	Body language
	Build
	Facial expressions
	Use of language
National	Flags
	Symbols
	Foods
	Architecture
	Music
Occupational	Uniforms
	Implements and props (stethoscope/doctor)
	Contexts
Corporate	Company logo
	Kind of advertising
	Headquarter buildings, etc.
	Product area
Gender	Clothes
	Hair style
	Voice
	Body structure
Religion	Symbols
	Clothes
	Objects
	Language
	Holy figures
	Architecture

Office Life

Executives Can Lose by a Hair

By Donald K. White, Business Editor

If you work in a Bay Area office or store and think your boss isn't aware of the way you wear your hair, guess again.

Even in this permissive area where off-beat hair styles, tight jeans with high heels on both women and men, and cowboy hats that have never been on the range are considered appropriate for business, many bosses don't agree.

In fact, many middle level executives in the Bay Area have been passed over for salary increases and promotions because their bosses didn't approve of their appearance but didn't have the nerve to tell them.

According to Linda Quigley, fashion coordinator for the 21 Command Performance hair styling stores in the Bay Area, at least one of every 12 male executives and one in 20 female executives wear their hair in styles that make them look weak and ineffective.

Quigley took a poll of 200 hair stylists and asked them to identify the worst ten hair styles worn by Bay Area executives, styles that even their best friends may never mention.

"Many executives are unaware of the negative messages they're sending out to their bosses by wearing their hair the wrong way," Quigley says. "Surprisingly it is the men who are the worst offenders."

Quigley's list of the five worst executive hair styles for men:

1) Crew Cut: Old-fashioned style indicates backward, sluggish thought processes and personal inflexibility. Rarely worn by younger men.

2) Hair parted to hide baldness: Conveys two undesirable leadership qualities—phoniness and self-consciousness.

3) Shoulder-length hair or hair that completely hides the collar: Upper management still perceives long hair on a man as indicative of anti-establishment values.

4) Greased hair: Looks too slick, gives impression that wearer also is too slick and untrustworthy.

5) Curly permanent that has grown out: A haggard looking style that conveys a sloppiness and disinterest.

As for women's business life hair styles:

1) Back-combed, bubbled or bouffant hair: Archaic, conveying lack of ability to embrace new concepts.

2) Feathered in front, long in back: Teeny-bopper style indicating lack of maturity, lack of professionalism.

3) Severely streaked hair: Creates image of cheapness, low morals and professional standards.

4) Long hair of one length all around: Plain Jane look suggesting lack of personality or warmth.

5) Punk rock hair: A contemporary hair style that conveys belligerence toward those in authority. (*San Francisco Examiner & Chronicle*, December 20, 1980.)

TEETH AS SIGNS

On the front page of *The Wall Street Journal* of June 16, 1982 there is an article by Marilyn Chase which is graced by a wonderful headline. It reads "Your Suit is Pressed, Hair Neat, but What Do Your Molars Say?" Describing a dental practice which treats teeth as signs she writes:

> A dental practice here (in San Francisco) is luring patients with a warning that people consciously or unconsciously "read" one another's teeth for clues to character....

Her attitude toward this phenomenon is that of disbelief and incredulity, for she sees this as "not unlike the way palm readers or phrenologists interpret lines on the hands or bumps on the head."

We are in the presence, we are led to believe, of one more bit of madness from California. Reporter Chase's tone is that of a bemused spectator detailing her experiences with a "hip" dentist, Dr. Jeffrey Morley, at his Center for Cosmetic Dentistry. Note her description of his office:

> The office's interior is California *grand luxe*, a sea of plush green carpet, green velour sofas, hanging plants, brass-trimmed butcher block and, of course, mirrors.

She quotes Morley on what teeth tell about people:

> "What it comes down to is this: Buck teeth imply people are dumb. Large canines imply aggressiveness. Weak chins imply passivity, while strong chins imply a macho, studly personality," he asserts. "I don't know who made these up, but the fact is, they're cultural standards."

In fact, Dr. Morley is quite correct in his assertion that teeth (and jaw formations) are "read" by people as indicators of personality. Given such a situation, there is a logic to doing something about problematical teeth, even though it may seem quite fantastic. Teeth are "read" as signs; indeed everything about a person is "read."

I have already said something about personal signs in my discussion of men's looks; obviously we only have signs to use to present ourselves to others, and these signs are all based on conventional understandings. Our clothes, hairstyles, and so on are the equivalent of stage props and are used to "broadcast," so to speak, our identities. Or, to be more precise, our personalities—remembering that the term *persona* means "mask."

Erving Goffman discusses this phenomenon in *The Presentation of Self in Everyday Life*:

...one may take the term "personal front" to refer to the other items of expressive equipment, the items that we most intimately identify with the performer himself and that we naturally expect will follow the performer wherever he goes. As part of personal front we may include: insignia of office or rank; clothing; sex, age, and racial characteristics; size and looks; posture; speech patterns; facial expressions; bodily gestures; and the like. (1959:23–24)

He points out that some sign vehicles, such as race, are fixed and don't vary from situation to situation but that others, such as facial expression, are quite mobile and do vary as situations change. In these performances we put on it is well to remember, as Goffman points out, that we are frequently taken in by ourselves.

National identity is integrally connected to symbols, flags, and other markers. If we wish to represent America by signs and symbols one thinks of such things as the Uncle Sam figure, of the American flag, of eagles, the Empire State Building, and the Grand Canyon, to name a few. The signs have all been continually used to represent America; some are natural phenomena, others are distinctive buildings, and others are symbols (like Uncle Sam) that have come to mean America. All have acquired their power to represent American nationality by continual use in the media, or (in the case of the flag) by historical circumstance.

When it comes to occupational identity, clothing, settings, and props are important and often several of these are needed to reinforce one another. Thus, a woman in a mini-skirt with a lot of cleavage showing is not necessarily anything. In one setting—a college campus, she might be just a sexy coed; in another setting, on a downtown street where "hookers" hang out, she quite probably will be a prostitute. People with distinctive occupations like to use settings and props to reinforce their identity claims. Thus college professors fill their offices with books. These books are signs of "scholarship" and are used, in part, for impression management, though they may also be used for writing and research. In fact, it is very difficult for most professionals to indicate their occupations nowadays since very few occupations have distinctive props to use. Settings, then, become the dominant way of indicating occupational identity.

Settings generate expectations and attitudes. Just as in the theater the setting gives us some kind of idea of what to expect, so it is in real life. People use settings to support their performances and legitimate their props. As in the theater, people take every object in a setting as a sign. The settings seem to make the props more powerful. Thus, in a hospital, a stethoscope has a more powerful meaning than it does, for example, in a regular room. The stethoscope is part of the technology of medicine and functions as a synechdochic object—a synechdoche occurs when a part or an aspect of something stands for the whole. In a hospital, surrounded (perhaps) by other objects and gadgets and machines, the stethoscope reminds one very directly of the vast and hugely expensive technological apparatus which doctors have at their command.

When we come to the matter of corporate identity we find ourselves in an area that has attracted much attention in recent years. One finds specialists in corporate identity now working in advertising agencies, design studies, marketing organizations, and related kinds of companies. Experts in corporate identity attempt to give people an impression of what a corporation is like through the use of logos, the use of certain typefaces, colors, and design features—all of which portray the company as it wishes to be portrayed.

Thus, in a letter (undated) by R. Burt Gookin, President and Chief Executive Officer of Heinz, we find the following:

> Even since its founding 100 years ago, H. J. Heinz Company has used a number of devices—the famed "57 Varieties," the keystone, the pickle and others—to identify itself and its products. Each of these devices has been effective in its time.
>
> The events of recent years have created a new and different company, however, and call for a new identification approach. The name "Heinz" now means Star-Kist, Ore-Ida, Plasmon, the Del Fuerte label in Mexico and the Teo label in Holland, among others. Moreover, "57 Varieties" is far wide of the mark today, when we make more than 1250 products.

Gookin then discusses how the corporation has spent two years in developing "a new corporate identifier [i.e., signifier] and a standardized system of corporate identification to serve our world-wide organization."

This letter, to Heinz World Management, is in the beginning of a notebook published in 1969, titled Heinz *Corporate Graphic Standards*, which deals, in great detail, with how the Heinz logo or "corporate mark" is to be used, what corporation stationery should look like, how the mark should be used in packaging, order forms, and so on. It even says what kind of paper (Strathmore Writing, White, Laid, Substance 24) should be used.

The Heinz corporate mark is, I find, a rather prosaic and uninteresting one that is probably perfectly suitable for a company that makes catsup and similar products. The mark used by Bank of America incorporates a bird into the design as a means of humanizing the organization and suggesting its power and transcendence. There is almost something feminine about the rounded nature of the letters forming the mark—the "A" curves up to a point from a solid base. Perhaps this mark is meant to soften the symbolism of the Bank of America headquarters in San Francisco, which is a huge, dark phallus-like structure that dominates the skyline and is vastly out of scale with the other buildings around it.

The use of letters to form a corporate mark is quite common, as an

Reprinted with permission of Heinz U.S.A., Pittsburgh.

The Heinz logo is one of the most familiar in the American food industry, and is probably very well suited for its intended audience.

examination of the symbols for companies such as Informatics General, Control Data, and Kimberly Clark shows. Other corporations use distinctive typography, symbolic animals, or unusual letter combinations (such as Exxon) to establish an identity. In some cases the symbology, typography, and so on are directly connected with the function of the corporation. Thus the Wells Fargo Bank plays upon the old Wells Fargo coaches and western themes. The bank has established such a connection between coaches, stage an auditory theme, and Wells Fargo, that it is not even necessary for the company to use its name now. When people hear the Wells Fargo theme and see stagecoaches, they know who is behind the commercial. Dreyfus asserts with its lion that it is king of the jungle, an apt metaphor for Wall Street, the stock market, and related financial areas.

All of these corporate marks attest to the arbitrary relation that exists between signifier (mark) and signified (corporation). As a rule they tend toward simplicity, the imaginative use of negative space, a kind of geometric formality and, in some cases, iconicity. In *Designing Corporate Symbols*, David E. Carter writes:

> A good corporate symbol doesn't just appear from nowhere. More often than not, a great deal of time, thought, and research go into the successful design.
>
> A good symbol accurately portrays the personality and function of the company. For every good corporate mark, there is a story behind it. (1975:9)

He then presents 148 corporate marks and quotes the designers of these marks, who tell about how they came to design the mark the way they did.

Some of the comments by the designers are rather terse and not terribly informative but others are quite interesting. One of the better discussions is given on the page describing the Crown Zellerbach logo:

> The Crown Zellerbach symbol is another example of abstracted company initials. The letters "C" and "Z" are formed by the white lines bisecting the

Reprinted with permission of Crown-Zellerbach, San Francisco.

black shape. It works as well in black and white as it does in color. When the symbol is used in the orange and red corporate colors, the "C" shape is orange separated by the diagonal white line from the red "Z" shape.

Another symbolic element present in the Crown Zellerbach mark is the abstract form of a roll of paper on a press. And paper is their business. Motion dynamics are quite strong in this symbol.

Designer: Robert Miles Runyan & Associates
Los Angeles, California (1975:52)

An examination of this mark shows that it is possible to pack a considerable amount of information into a relatively simple symbol. The Crown Zellerbach symbol is both an abstraction, formed by the company letters, and an icon of the company's function. I think it is an extremely successful mark which is both interesting, visually, and functional: it suggests dynamism and also portrays the use of paper.

Gender identity is one of the more confused and complicated topics we have to deal with. In the 1960s and 70s it became difficult to tell gender on the basis of clothes, hair style, names, and so on. There was a big unisex movement that attempted to blur gender distinctions. It still has adherents, even as I write, in various places in America and elsewhere. It isn't too unusual to see a male with long hair, a highly decorative shirt and pants, who—from a distance or perhaps from the rear—might be mistaken for a woman. Likewise, many women now have short hair, wear business-type suits (even, in some cases with ties) and have a decidedly masculine look.

The rise of moustaches and beards in recent years may have something to do with an attempt, on the part of many men, to assert their masculinity in the face of all the attacks on male identity mounted by both the unisex movement and the women's liberation movement. These attacks, I should point out, were on stereotypes and sexist attitudes many men held relative to male identity rather than on male identity, per se. In any case, the unisex movement no longer threatens to become dominant and gender differentiation is now more marked. Women's fashions in 1982, for example, no longer feature the exaggerated shoulders and other hyper-masculine features which were popular just a few years ago. (The football player in his shoulder-pads would be the archetype of hypermasculine fashion.)

Gay fashion seems to be influential now, especially in the current look—short hair and a beard (or thick moustache). What gay men are searching for, as I understand it, is masculinity; thus long hair, which traditionally has been equated with femininity, would not be desirable. Hence beards and short hair—a look that the straight community is now adopting.

Religious identity is an area in which great differentiation is accomplished by the use of specific kinds of clothes, objects, and symbols. Different religious groups adopt various "uniforms" which signify that one is an adherent of a particular religion—or branch of that religion. Thus we have the Roman collar which, when worn with a black suit, usually indicates the Roman Catholic faith and which, when worn with an ordinary suit, suggests the Protestant faith. Most religions have articulated very specific kinds of garments for specific functions and use clothing as a means of both separating themselves from others and generating group cohesion.

Thus we find adherents of various Buddhist sects wearing robes, we find Orthodox Jews wearing Yarmulkas and Tsit-tsits (fringed garments), Catholic nuns wearing habits, and so on. There are different habits that nuns wear, depending upon the order they belong to (though, in recent years, many nuns in America have abandoned the practice of wearing habits). Likewise, Chassidic Jews (who are Orthodox but differ from ordinary Orthodox Jews) wear long black coats, strange fur hats, and so on. The only difference between ordinary fashion and religious fashion is that the latter is highly articulated, formalized, and nonchanging. The essence of religious fashion is nonmutability and precise meaning. If you believe there is a divine command that you dress in a certain way and do certain things with certain objects, you are not likely to be interested in change for change's sake.

Two aspects of identity are considered in the review of Return of the Jedi *that follows: first, the film is, in many respects a fairy tale with numerous mythic and folkloristic overtones and second, that its themes are very much connected to the American value system.*

THE REWARDS OF MYTH*

Return of the Jedi, in the first two months after its release, grossed more than two-hundred million dollars. And the *Star Wars* trilogy, on an investment of approximately 60 million dollars, has returned more than a billion dollars. The amount of money these films are making simply boggles the mind. We are not just dealing with films here, but with a phenomenon of awesome proportions, for in addition to the films, there are all the spinoffs to consider: records, toys, games, "figures," etc.

When a film such as *Return of the Jedi* succeeds the way it has, it must, somehow, do things for people, provide important gratifications, reassurances, fantasies...whatever you will. It is not enough to say that the film entertains. That word tells us nothing. It is what the entertainment does to people—and for them—that is of interest.

Many critics have commented that *Return of the Jedi*, like its predecessors, is a fairy tale. It has, like the classic old fairy tales, a young hero who survives numerous ordeals and, with the aid of various helpers, triumphs. This hero is often "twinned," and in *Jedi* we discover that Princess Leia is Luke Skywalker's sister, no less...which means that we have two Jedi figures instead of one. (This is a nod to women's liberation and also sets the stage for future heroic activities by Leia.)

Luke has sidekicks—Leia, Han, Chewbacca, See-Threepio, Artoo-Detoo—and, more importantly, tutelary figures. Thus we find Yoda, and

* Published by permission of Transaction Inc. From *Society*. Copyright © 1983 by Transaction Inc.

before him, Obi Ben Kenobi, who help Luke transform himself from a raw youth, full of potential, into an actual Jedi knight. To achieve knighthood, Luke must "confront" his father, Darth Vader, in a classically Oedipal battle. They fight with light sabers (phalluses) as a hideous and vaguely sexually ambivalent emperor looks on, urging Luke to kill his father and take his place as the Emperor's minion. The magic light saber reminds one, of course, of King Arthur's sword Excalibur.

One important theme in fairy tales involves finding magic helpers who ultimately come to the aid of the hero and his friends. Thus in the redwood forest we find Ewoks, little teddy bear-like figures who also happen to be fierce and ingenious warriors. They live in a magic kingdom high in the trees (echoes of Swiss Family Robinson here?).

Like the classic fairy tale, *Return of the Jedi* has a "happy ending." This is necessary to give the young child, who is using the fairy tale to learn about life and gain courage, a sense that he or she has possibilities, can triumph even though the odds (small child versus big dragons, monsters, evil kings) seem hopeless. Thus Luke ultimately "redeems" his father, via the power of love, by forcing his father to triumph over the spirit of evil that has dominated him. As Luke writhes on the ground, immobilized by the electric flashes emanating from the evil Emperor, Luke makes his father renounce evil. Blood is thicker than brainwashing. When Darth Vader seizes the Emperor, lifts him high over his head and throws him down an almost endless pit, Vader's long period of domination by evil is ended and he can die "heroically." With his death and the destruction of the evil empire, the picture ends and so does the trilogy. One of the interesting features of *Return of the Jedi* is the way it incorporates various pop culture genres in it. Pop ontogeny recapitulates pop phylogeny in Lucas films...and may account, in part, for their popularity. All the special effects in the world don't matter if you don't have a good narrative and themes with which audiences can identify.

The first part of the film, which dragged a good deal as far as I'm concerned, had caveman film elements in it. Thus the monster kept in the dungeon beneath Jabba the Hut's castle seemed like something from a prehistoric caveman epic. Also the mechanical monsters guarding the empire's outpost were, obviously, dinosaurs. And even the setting for the adventure in the woods had a kind of primeval "this is the way the world was in the beginning" ring to it. One cannot help but notice the paradisical aspects of the marvelous forest in which much of the action took place.

There are also strong elements of the samurai film here, except that instead of Toshiro Mifune destroying a town full of villains with his flashing sword, Luke devastates Jabba's army with his light saber. If you think about it, there is something incongrous about having a sword in a high-tech laser-beam world...except that swordplay has a dramatic power to it that gunplay doesn't. The classic battle, of course, was between Luke and his father—a battle that Luke was predestined to win. In fairy tales the young boy must triumph over his father (or father figure) in order to make possible the child's separation and individualization.

And, of course, there was the battle scene between the rebels and the empire, which is a redoing of the Old World War II American-German dogfights and attacks. (The faces and uniforms of people in the empire have a distinctly Germanic flavor. This was particularly evident in *Star Wars*.) In *Return of the Jedi* the Death Star seemed all-powerful and then, suddenly, incredibly vulnerable to the rebel attack. Once Luke and his friends had destroyed the station that kept the Death Star protected, finishing off the thing was quite easy. I found the battle scene a bit déja vu, I must admit. This one had more special effects than the one in *Star Wars*, but it seemed to be rather routine and even, perhaps, a bit mechanical. There may be an element of technological overkill in these battles.

One of the reasons *Return of the Jedi* is so popular is that it has a rather clearcut series of oppositions in it that give it meaning. Thus we find the following oppositions in the story:

Youth	Old Age
Luke	The Emperor
Nature	Technology
Forest	Death Star
The Force	Evil
The Rebels	The Empire
Freedom	Tyranny
Love	Hate
Good Beasts	Bad Beasts
Ewoks	Jabba
The Son	The Father

These oppositions help make the fairy tale understandable to viewers and provide them with easy objects to identify with or despise. Only Darth Vader is complicated, for he moves from seeming to be evil incarnate to relative goodness when put to the test. Perhaps a bit too quickly, as a matter of fact.

Finally, the thematic structure of *Return of the Jedi* is congruent with our belief structure, so the film has the benefit of both providing a kind of escape and, at the same time, of reinforcing our sacred values. *Return of the Jedi* may be popular all over the world but its value system is quintessentially American. First, we find youth triumphing and, what is more, teaching adults about love and goodness. This notion that young people are, somehow, wiser and perhaps even nobler than adults, is particularly American.

The second important theme involves faith in oneself. That is what

Luke needs—actually all he needs—to become a full-fledged Jedi knight. In America we used to call it willpower. In a society in which we believe we all have equal opportunity (since we have, we believe, no rigid class system, no aristocracy, etc.) success is essentially a function of effort and faith in oneself. This is behind what is sometimes called the middle-class "effort-optimism" syndrome.

At the end of *Return of the Jedi*, Luke has control of the Force (read phallus and his sexuality here), his father is dead but "redeemed" by his son before dying, the empire is crushed once again (but for how long we ask?) and the second trilogy in a nine-film epic has concluded. The stage is set, in the first three films, for Darth Vader to succumb to evil, and in the last three films for Princess Leia to do a Joan of Arc number.

There were a number of unfavorable reviews of *Return of the Jedi*. The film was criticized for being too violent, too formulaic, too predictable, boring, etc. And George Lucas (Luke-as Skywalker) is, so we hear, tired of it all. The reviews may not be so hot but the box office is doing very well, and that's what counts, ultimately, in show business. It seems unlikely that the *Star Wars* epic will not be continued. It is too valuable a commercial property to let die. Whether all the special effects will continue to dazzle people and the plots continue to interest them—in the years, perhaps even decades to come—remains to be seen.

Fourteen

Terms Associated with Signs

In *Webster's Ninth New Collegiate Dictionary* there are over 20 different definitions of "sign" and more than 40 words related to the word "sign." This, in itself, is a sign of the complexity and multidimensionality of the concept. I will consider, below, some related words that I think are particularly interesting.

1. *Signature.* A person's name-sign. In some cases the signature is almost illegible which indicates that the mark function has become more important than the naming function. We seldom think about it but to a large degree our name is our sign and our signature is our distinctive way of writing this sign. This is particularly important in situations where a number of people have the same name. In a small city such as San Francisco there are dozens of John Smiths, and so on. For such people it is their signature, not their name, which is the distinctive sign of their existence.

We also use the term "signature" to stand for idiosyncratic and distinctive aspects of an artist's style. What *auteur* film critics search for is, in essence, an authorial signature. This is what Geoffrey Nowell-Smith meant when he described *auteur* theory (quoted in Wollen, 1972:80):

¹sign \'sin\ *n* [ME *signe,* fr. OF, fr. L *signum* mark, token, sign, image, seal; prob. akin to L *secare* to cut — more at SAW] (13c) **1 a :** a motion or gesture by which a thought is expressed or a command or wish made known **b :** SIGNAL 2a **c :** a fundamental linguistic unit that designates an object or relation or has a purely syntactic function **d :** one of a set of gestures used to represent language; *also :* SIGN LANGUAGE **2 :** a mark having a conventional meaning and used in place of words or to represent a complex notion **3 :** one of the 12 divisions of the zodiac **4 a** (1) **:** a character (as a flat or sharp) used in musical notation (2) **:** SEGNO **b :** a character (as ÷) indicating a mathematical operation; *also :* one of two characters + and − that form part of the symbol of a number and characterize it as positive or negative **5 a :** a lettered board or other display used to identify or advertise a place of business **b :** a posted command, warning, or direction **c :** SIGNBOARD **6 a :** something material or external that stands for or signifies something spiritual **b :** something indicating the presence or existence of something else ⟨∼s of success⟩ ⟨a ∼ of the times⟩ **c :** PRESAGE, PORTENT ⟨∼s of an early spring⟩ **d :** an objective evidence of plant or animal disease **7** *pl usu* **sign :** traces of a usu. wild animal ⟨red fox ∼⟩ — **signed** *adj*
    syn SIGN, MARK, TOKEN, NOTE, SYMPTOM mean a discernible indication of what is not itself directly perceptible. SIGN applies to any indication to be perceived by the senses or the reason; MARK suggests something impressed on or inherently characteristic of a thing often in contrast to general outward appearance; TOKEN applies to something that serves as a proof of something intangible; NOTE suggests a distinguishing mark or characteristic; SYMPTOM suggests an outward indication of an internal change or condition.
²sign *vb* [ME *signen,* fr. MF *signer,* fr. L *signare* to mark, sign, seal, fr. *signum*] *vt* (14c) **1 a :** to place a sign on **b :** CROSS 2 **c :** to represent or indicate by a sign **2 a :** to affix a signature to : ratify or attest by hand or seal ⟨∼ a bill into law⟩ ⟨the prisoner ∼ed a confession⟩ **b :** to assign or convey formally ⟨∼ed over his property to his brother⟩ **c :** to write down (one's name) **3 :** to communicate by making a sign or by sign language **4 :** to engage or hire by securing the signature of on a contract of employment — often used with *up* or *on* ∼ *vi* **1 :** to write one's name in token of assent, responsibility, or obligation **2 a :** to make a sign or signal **b :** to use sign language — **sign·ee** \ˌsi-'nē\ *n* — **sign·er** \'si-nər\ *n*

By permission. From Webster's Ninth New Collegiate Dictionary © 1983 by Merriam-Webster, Inc., Publishers of the Merriam-Webster® Dictionaries.

A typical dictionary has many different definitions for the word "sign."

One essential corollary of the theory as it has been developed is the discovery that the defining characteristics of an author's work are not necessarily those which are the most readily apparent. The purpose of criticism thus becomes to uncover behind the superficial contrasts of subject and treatment a hard core of basic and often recondite motifs. The pattern formed by these motifs... is what gives an author's work its particular structure, both defining it internally and distinguishing one body of work from another.

I have, perhaps, stretched the concept of signature a bit here, but I believe it is really what *auteur* criticism is about. Signature presupposes, of course, a distinctive and personal style—what might be described as a well-developed aesthetic personality.

2. *Resign.* This comes from the Latin *resignare,* to unseal or cancel, but more likely or more directly, to give up the signs of office, and to indicate doing so by offering a signed statement (usually). Since political office, rank in corporations, and so on are accompanied by various signs, to resign is to let go of these signs. Signs of the presidency are such things as the White House, Air Force Number One, and so on.

There is another meaning to the word "resign," which involves the acceptance of what cannot be avoided or postponed. Often this resignation comes after a considerable amount of effort and hard work—which is unsuccessful. Then one submits to fate with resignation, since all other options are closed.

It is worth noting that sometimes it takes a great deal of hard work to get a political figure to become "resigned" to his fate and to resign. The resignation of Richard Nixon from the presidency is a case in point. It took an enormous amount of pressure to pry him out of the Oval Office and send him packing to California.

3. *Insignia.*   Insignia are signs of rank in an organization that is hierarchically structured. (The term comes from the Latin *insigne*, mark or badge.) In order to interpret insignia correctly, one must have recourse to some code book, which tells how the insignia are to be read. In other words, there must be a formal sign system and people must be taught it. In the military, insignia are functional in that they are ways of demonstrating authority. In a battle they are dysfunctional, in that the enemy can destroy the command system by killing officers; frequently insignia are removed (temporarily) to confuse the enemy.

4. *Design.*   To give form or shape to signs—or, perhaps, to turn objects and artifacts into signs. A designer manipulates shape, size, color, etc. so as to generate desired meanings and emotions. Design usually implies some kind of aesthetic dimension. Thus, for example, there was the designer-jeans phenomenon in America (and elsewhere) in recent years. These jeans were more expensive than ordinary jeans and usually carried designer labels (signs) to differentiate them from run-of-the-mill jeans . . . and the people who wore such jeans.

To be manufactured an object has to be designed; that goes without saying. But some objects are produced for the lowest price and for the largest (some would say lowest) common denominator, while others are produced with more attention to aesthetics and less concern with saving money. The taste of the designer becomes, then, an important aspect of the object.

5. *Significant.*   This is a sign that is important, that represents something worth considering, that tells us something worth knowing. To coin a phrase, "all signs are important, but some signs are more important than others." When we use the term "significant," we are, in fact, functioning as semiologists—even though we may not be aware of the fact. We are making a dichotomy among signs: some are significant and others are insignificant. But in all cases it is signs with which we are dealing.

The word "auteur" means "author" in English. "Auteur" criticism attempts to determine who is the most important person in collaborative art forms such as films (where one finds producers, directors, writers, etc.), television programs, and other areas. Here I focus on the matter of an artist's "signature" or personal stamp.

DIRECTORIAL SIGNATURE IN FILM:
A CONSIDERATION OF AUTEUR THEORY

Film is a collaborative art form in which a number of people, with different areas of expertise, play an important role. There are actors and actresses who are performance artists; there are film editors, film music writers, camera operators, costume directors, lighting experts, and a number of other people who might be classified as production artists; and there is a producer who takes care of the financing of the film and a writer (or several) who create the screenplay. Then, first among equals, at the very least, there is the director. It is the director who, in the final analysis, is responsible for the film turning out the way it does.

In recent years, with the development of *auteur* criticism, film critics have started paying increasing attention to the role of the director and have become interested in what might be called "directorial signature," the stylistic and thematic aspects of the director's corpus of works which are distinctive and personal.

An excellent description of *auteur* criticism is found in Joseph M. Boggs' *The Art of Watching Films*. He writes:

> In this approach we focus on the style, technique, and philosophy of the film's dominant creative personality—the director who acts as an *auteur*...a complete filmmaker whose genius, style, and creative personality are reflected in

every aspect of the film. Since all truly great directors impose their personalities on every aspect of their films the film is viewed not as an objective work of art but as a reflection of the person who made it, especially in terms of his or her artistic vision or style. A good movie according to this theory is therefore one which bears the trademark of the director and reflects the personality of a single creative genius in every element—the story, the casting, the cinematography, the lighting, the music, the sound effects, the editing, and so on. And the film must not be judged alone, but as part of the whole canon of the director's works. (1978:245–246)

The focus in *auteur* criticism, then, is upon that which is distinctive in a director's body of work and it is, in essence, a historical approach wedded to considerations of stylistic identity or what I have called "signature." This approach is very similar to that used by literary scholars who write books about an author's development and analyze his or her major works. The only difference is that film is a collaborative art form and it is difficult to assign "authorship" to the director the way we can to the writer.

For a discussion of directorial style, focusing on technical or aesthetic aspects, I would like to offer a series of quotations from V. F. Perkins' essay, "The Cinema of Nicholas Ray." Ray directed films such as *Run for Cover, Hot Blood, Party Girl, The James Brothers, King of Kings, They Live by Night, Wind Across the Everglades* and *Rebel Without a Cause*. The quotations will show the kinds of things Perkins is interested in as he attempts to show what is distinctive and characteristic in Ray's films.

1. *Action.* Throughout any Ray movie one finds a complete mastery of the—often contradictory—action which expresses more that it does, the ability to convey an idea through a gesture, a hesitation, a movement of the eyes.

2. *Framing.* Ray frequently uses static masses with bold lines—walls, staircases, doors, rocks—which intrude into the frame and at the same time disrupt and unify his images. In particular he uses objects in order to enclose his characters, to produce a frame within the frame.

3. *Editing.* . . . a Ray movie is instantly recognizable as such by the director's extremely individual use of editing. Many of Ray's camera movements appear to be incomplete. Any simple guide to movie-making will tell you that a travelling shot must have a beginning, middle and end. Often Ray uses only the middle: the camera is already moving at the beginning of the shot, and the movement is unfinished when the next shot appears.

4. *Symbolization.* The desire for direct communication also distinguishes Ray's use of symbolism. His images are never obscure; many of them are derived from nature, like the references to fire and water in *King of Kings*, or to rock and wind in *Johnny Guitar*. . . . (Quoted in Nichols, 1976:253, 255–256)

From these quotations you can see Ray's concerns as a director and what Perkins believes to be important. If one has not seen a large number of films by Ray it is difficult to ascertain how correct Perkins is in his analysis, though he does cite events and scenes in various Ray films in the article.

The other school of *auteur* criticism is more interested in themes and sociopolitical motifs in a director's work than in aesthetic and technical issues. Thus Peter Wollen's treatment of directors such as Howard Hawks and John Ford deals with their thematic preoccupations and constantly recurring incidents and motifs.

In *Signs and Meaning in the Cinema*, Wollen discusses an important aspect of Ford's work:

> Ford finds transcendent values in the historic vocation of America as a nation, to bring civilization to a savage land, the garden to the wilderness. At the same time, Ford also sees these values themselves as problematic. (1972:81)

This opposition between the garden and the wilderness is, for Wollen, "the master antinomy in Ford's films," and explains Ford's fascination (if not preoccupation) with the quest theme—the search for the Promised Land, "an American re-enactment of the Biblical exodus, the journey through the desert to the land of milk and honey, the New Jerusalem." (1972:97)

Wollen points out that although Hawks directed films in every genre, he reduces all these genres to two kinds of films: adventure dramas and crazy comedies. In his adventure dramas, "the highest human emotion is the camaraderie of the exclusive, self-sufficient, all-male group." Hawks' heroes all, Wollen says, must pass tests of ability to be admitted to this desired group. Their allegiance to the group and its security is sacred and the members of the group bind themselves together by rituals.

The comedies are different. Here the dominant themes are regression to childhood and infantilism and "sex-reversal and role-reversal" in films which are centered around "domineering women and timid, pliable men." In the dramas men are heroic and triumph over nature; in the comedies they are victims and weaklings, or the polar opposites of what they were in the adventure films.

Wollen's concerns, it can be seen, are very different from a writer like Perkins. *Auteur* criticism for Wollen is cultural, sociological, political, and psychological (or psychoanalytic). It is not terribly interested in technique and aesthetic considerations. Instead it focuses attention on content and theme—though still in the context of a particular director's work. I would suggest that both form and content, technique and theme, are important. Rather than choosing one or the other, it makes sense to examine both aspects of a director's work and, in addition, to consider the relationship that exists between stylistic technique and meaning.

What "signs" are characteristic of a director's work and how do these "signs" affect the themes that preoccupy him or her? This seems to be a much more interesting question than trying to decide whether the aestheticians or the ideologues (to put the argument in extremes) are right.

Fifteen

Signs and Images

Signs are generally composed of a number of different elements, each of which itself may function as a sign. Some signs, of course, are extremely simple—such as an arrow indicating where one should go to arrive at a desired destination. But most signs are much more complicated than that, and we usually find ourselves with a number of things to consider in the analysis of a sign.

Let me suggest some terms we might use in dealing with signs so that when I use a word we will know precisely what I have in mind. We will proceed from the simple to the complicated.

Signemes or Sign Elements. These are the most fundamental elements in a sign, elements that cannot be broken down further. They are the most simple signs. A bubble in a glass of champagne would be a sign element or signeme. So would the light yellow color champagne has.

Signs. Signs are more complex than signemes and might be called complex signs, except that it is a bit unwieldly to use that term all the time. We define a sign as something which stands (or can be made to stand) for

114

something else or which can be used to stand for something else. Signs are collections of signemes. Thus, a champagne bottle is a sign that contains many different sign elements: wire, gold foil, a label, and so on.

Icon.   An icon is a collection of visual signs, as in a photograph, a frame from a film, a "still" from a television program, an advertisement, etc. An icon, such as a photograph, might show people wearing certain clothes or costumes in certain settings doing certain activities: and all of these phenomena are signs which can be read for meaning.

Sign Assemblage.   This is a collection of signs of an auditory as well as visual nature that occurs in a relatively short passage of time. I wish to have a way of considering sound effects and music as signs in specific situations and I am using sign assemblage for this purpose. A sign assemblage is part of a narrative or text.

Text.   This is a term which is used, conventionally, to mean a systematically related collection of signs in a narrative, such as a film, television program, play, and so on. We use it, loosely, to mean "the subject of our analysis" (which means that newspaper and magazine advertisements also are texts, though relatively simple texts). Thus, the CBS National News, *Raiders of the Lost Ark*, poems, a Burger King commercial, *A Passage to India*, an advertisement in *Playboy*, songs, as well as descriptive, expository, and argumentative materials, are all texts, though some are more complex and challenging than others.

This system of categories or definitions has deficiencies, but it does allow us to discuss signs more systematically and with more specificity.

Let me offer an example of how these terms might be used in the analysis of a wedding as a text.

Signeme/Sign Elements	Bubbles in champagne
Sign	Champagne bottle
Icon	Photograph of bride and groom drinking champagne
Sign Assemblage	Sounds and smells, when photograph was being snapped
Text	The wedding itself, from beginning to end

A champagne bottle is a rather complex sign, made up of signemes such as foil, wire, a label, a certain brand name (which is an indicator of the quality, cost, or value of the champagne itself), a yellow wine, bubbles, etc.—all of which might be analyzed.

Why, we might ask, do we have champagne at weddings and other celebrations? One reason might be that good champagne is relatively

Photograph by Jan Browman

Champagne.

expensive, so serving champage is an indicator of one's wealth (and power) and that one wants to give one's guests the "very best." Champagne is also full of life and vitality; it has bubbles that signify these things. Champagne is sparkling and effervescent. When we drink champagne we "take in" this life and make it part of ourselves. Good champagne is also quite delicious and has the virtue of going with almost all dishes. So it is champagne we drink at weddings, at Bar Mitzvahs, at festive parties...champagne to signify taste, to signify class, to signify life.

There is also something sexual about the way champagne spurts out of its bottle which is another reason champagne is used at weddings. Champagne functions as a kind of metaphor for sexual relations; it is not for nothing (as Alan Dundes has pointed out) that the bride throws a bouquet of flowers away, symbolizing the fact that she is to be "deflowered." Opening a bottle of champagne is, then, a symbolic rehearsal of male orgasm.

Technically, only wine made in the Champagne region of France can

*You are cordially invited to be
included among a limited number of
United States citizens
privileged to receive one of the world's most
colorful and exciting publications.*

RSVP

Details inside

Reprinted with permission of *Soviet Life*, 1706 Eighteenth Street, N.W., Washington, D.C. 20009.

be called champagne. But now champagne has become an appelation used for an entire genre of sparkling white wines. So, in one sense, champagne is a case-study in the appropriation of a sign, and champagne-style wines are now neither rare nor expensive—though fine champagne is both.

Analyzing a Russian Image   The illustration we are examining comes from an advertisement for *Soviet Life*, a monthly magazine distributed in America by the Russians. What is interesting about this image? How does it signify "Russianness" and what does it tell us about Russia?

Note the printed matter, which is both humble and somewhat elitist. We are "cordially invited" to be among a "limited number" of citizens of the United States "privileged" to purchase the magazine. The type face is somewhat formal and balanced, suggesting an invitation to some occasion of importance. The appeal is to elitist and somewhat nondemocratic aspects of our collective personality—due, no doubt, to the fact that we are a "bourgeois" society.

Look, now, at that wondrous leap of the dancer—the expression of exhilaration on his face, the energy and enthusiasm he reflects. This is the "old" Russia of peasants and fantastic dancers that we all think so fondly of, a Russia that is quaint and colorful. Note also the way his arms and legs are stretched horizontally. There are four horizontal bands in this photograph: the dancer's arms, his legs, the line of Russian women and the line of Russian men, whose interlocked arms suggest their brotherhood and sense of equality.

The photograph is a study in the equality of man, of the brotherhood of man, of the charm of Russia, and of its energy. This, we are led to believe, is the real Russia. There are no tanks and soldiers invading Czechoslovakia or Afganistan here. (That is a fantasy of the American government and the lackey news organizations.)

Reinforcing all this is the costuming, which suggests some kind of ethnic, folk subgroup. The shirts are, it seems, embroidered with a floral pattern, further reinforcing the natural, quaint, old-fashioned, peasant-like message of the advertisement. This photograph returns us to the mythological Russia of our fantasies—happy peasants freed from serfdom and ecstatic on collectivized farms, dancing with joy. Equally important is what the photograph does *not* show in its attempts to give people an image of Russia. We must always speculate, when confronted with a sign or a collection of signs or an image, why this image and why not something else?

Photography has evolved from being a curiosity to being an important art form. How does one interpret a photograph? How does one discover all that a photograph contains? When we define a photograph as an icon full of signs and signifiers we are on our way to a more refined and complex means of interpreting it.

PHOTOGRAPHY

The photograph has come a long way since 1826 when photography was born. Nicéphore Niépce's picture of a view from his window is often cited as the first photograph. It is a crude and grainy shot of a garden. Since that time our technology and our attitudes toward photography have changed considerably. We now have cameras that don't use film, cameras that produce photographs just seconds after we have snapped the shutter, and disc cameras which promise (in the advertisements) "decision-free" photography.

As the camera has changed from a crude machine to a gadget to a highly sophisticated device, our conceptions of photography have also evolved. It is fair to say that photography is now seen by many critics as an art form of major importance. Prints of great photographs by masters such as Ansel Adams and Diane Arbus now sell for thousands of dollars, and there are presently numerous art galleries devoted only to photography.

There is developing a body of criticism, also, including works such as Susan Sontag's *On Photography* and Roland Barthes's *Camera Lucida*. One important notion of many critics interested in photography is that the photograph is not just a simple reflection of reality. Thus Howard S. Becker writes in an essay, "Aesthetics and Truth:"

When people make or use photographs for scientific or scholarly purposes, they do not strive for unique visions or personal styles. Instead, they want material that helps them answer a question taken seriously in an established community concerned with such questions. Such photographs are frequently made in a standardized fashion, so accepted in the user community that its members think it the only way such pictures can be made. But every choice embodied in those images—of framing, lens, lighting, printing—is a choice that could have been made differently, with a different photographic result. (*Society*, July/August 1980:27–28)

What Becker points out is that there are all kinds of aesthetic decisions to be made in even the most straightforward shot. The camera does not run by itself or, as Becker puts it, "photographs do not record reality neutrally."

The photographer, in a sense, creates the reality of the photograph. This "reality" is affected by the lighting to a great degree. Strong lighting, which negates shadows and imparts a two-dimensionality to the persons or objects being photographed, yields a very different effect than soft lighting. The chiascuro effect, in which there are strong lights and darks, conveys a different attitude to the viewer from flat lighting or other kinds of lighting. And lighting is only one of the components of the photograph.

(The idea that the camera merely reflects reality is responsible for the notion many people have that television always tells the truth. People believe this because, as they tell you, "seeing is believing." What people do not think about—and this applies equally to still photographs—is that what they see on television is what someone wants them to see. Sometimes what the television camera doesn't show is more important than what it does. The camera always records a particular person's perspective or point of view which may be part of the truth but not all the truth.)

In short, there is much room for judgment in the taking of photographs and in the making of the photographs. Every photograph reflects a number of things about the photographer who took it: his or her technical ability, aesthetic sensibility, social and political orientation, and values, to name some of the more important considerations.

Just as the photograph reflects what the photographer knows, what we see in a photograph reflects what we know. What we know, believe, and are affects what we get out of a given photograph. As John Berger writes in *Ways of Seeing*, "the way we see things is affected by what we know or what we believe." (1972:8) (Sociologists often discuss the same thing when they talk about selective perception and selective inattention—the way people see only what they want to see and don't see what they don't wish to see.)

Photographs are one important form of image, for Berger, which he defines as a "sight which has been recreated or reproduced." He adds, "It is an appearance, or a set of appearances, which has been detached from the place and time in which it first made its appearance and preserved—for a few moments or a few centuries." (1972:9, 10) These images provide "direct testimony about the world which surrounded other people at other times," and thus are of value to the social historian—even though the "way of seeing" of the photographer must be taken into account. We must also take into account the ways of seeing of the people at large—their assumptions about reality, the good life, beauty, taste, and so on.

For the average person, a photograph is a way of capturing a moment in time and preserving it. People take photographs at events of special meaning to them: weddings, bar mitzvahs, parties, and convocations, for example. It is as if some kind of a visual image were required to certify that something happened. These photos have an existential significance. They say, "look, we exist!" And when we take photographs of ourselves in front of monuments, cathedrals in France, with natives in exotic lands, we are preserving a record of our exploits. "Look," say these photographs, "I've had adventures, I've seen things, I've done things." (I'm making a distinction here between snapshots of ourselves on our travels and portraits that we take which usually do not show us doing anything, but just being ourselves.)

In his essay, "The Image-Freezing Machine," Stanley Milgram points out that photographs not only create their own reality but also often affect reality. He writes:

> There is a universe of events that we smell and a universe that we hear; there is also a universe of events whose existence is embodied in photographs. Thus each year we eagerly await the official Chinese Communist May Day photograph to see who is photographed alongside the chairman and who has been displaced. The official photograph is not only a reflection of the political reality, but itself solidifies that reality and becomes and element in it. The question, therefore, is to what degree events that exist in photographs exert an effect outside the photograph. Does a photograph act back on and shape the real world? (*Society,* November/December, 1976:12)

Milgram's answer to this question is "yes!" The photograph has a double valence: it both reflects and affects reality.

The photographic image permeates our culture. There are photographs in our books, magazines, newspapers, on the walls of our houses, on billboards, in advertising of all sorts. We are bombarded by so many photographs that we seldom take a moment to examine them and consider the reality they present to us and the effects they may be having upon us. It might be worthwhile examining them carefully, taking them seriously.

Sixteen

No Sign as Sign

No sign is also a sign. Since we are sign-giving and sign-interpreting animals and since for much of our lives we are involved with this kind of activity, no signs or absent signs (where signs are expected) also communicate something to us. Let me suggest some areas where a lack of signs is a sign, and say a bit about what these absent signs reveal.

Area	Meaning
Phone rings but caller says nothing	Prankster, pervert, or wrong number and embarrassment
Dog not barking at murderer	Master revealed as killer
No response to stimuli	Catatonic
Not doing what is expected of you	Aggressive passivity
No brain waves	Dead
No reply to letter	Rejection, lack of decision, letter misplaced

One of the few laws that social scientists seem to have discovered about people is that the "law of reciprocity" usually operates. We tend to feel that we should *get* an amount equal to what we *give* (though there are, I admit, aberrations such as the potlatch), that we should be treated fairly and justly. Closely allied to this principle is the matter of feedback. We feel that when we give a sign to someone, such as saying "hello," we should get an appropriate response—some form of greeting or reply. When we don't get the response we expect, we take it as a sign of something. Saying nothing can speak volumes.

It isn't always possible to determine what "absent" signs mean—when we get a phone call and nobody answers, it could be a pervert or a criminal calling to see whether anyone is home. But it also could be someone who got a wrong number, recognized that the voice answering the phone was wrong, and simply hung up. When a person doesn't say anything and doesn't hang up, then we know something fishy is going on and should, so people from the phone company tell us, hang up immediately.

The dog *not* barking during a murder is a different sort of thing. Here it is important to recognize that the dog *should* have been barking—since, presumably, dogs bark at strangers—so when the dog doesn't bark, that becomes a sign of something. Or, to be more precise, someone—namely the dog's owner or someone the dog knows.

Not doing anything when something is expected of you is a form of hostile behavior labeled "passive aggression" by some and "aggressive passivity" by others. Passive–aggressive people are angry and express this anger by not doing their fair share which, usually, leads to a response by others who adopt the same tactics. This kind of behavior tears relationships apart, because the partners in the passive–aggressive scenario keep mounting the stakes, keep refusing to do more and more of what is expected of them so that eventually, without striking a blow, they come to hate one another. What makes this so insidious is that nothing *seems* to be happening; a wife keeps putting off mending something for her husband, a husband "forgets" to pick up something his wife asked him to get at the supermarket, and so on. Before long, conscious and unconscious resentments poison the relationship and we are left with people who have literally done *nothing* to one another—with vengeance.

What does it mean, I ask in this essay, to have a "natural look?" Isn't this a contradiction in terms? I argue here that nature is a crucial concept in American culture and that a "natural" look conveys important meanings to people. The "natural look" must be seen in the context of other "artificial" looks and as an affirmation of American idealism and utopianism as well as anxiety about sexuality.

THE NATURAL LOOK: (NO MAKEUP)

The natural look is best described in terms of what it is not—it is a "look" in which no makeup is used, no lipstick, no eye shadow, no cosmetics of any kind. It is based on the rejection of cosmetics, of that which is "artificial" and contrived. It is only meaningful, then, in the context of a beauty system in which, at one pole, there is glamour and cosmetics, and at the other pole, diametrically opposed, there is beauty and naturalness.

Nature is an important word in the American mind. Whether it is true or not, we see ourselves (and have done so for centuries) as living in nature in contrast to the Europeans (in particular) who we see as living in history and having culture, institutions, and other resources that go with this circumstance. We stress our natural state and its concomitants: purity, honesty, simplicity, and so on.

Thus the natural look, which is a contradiction in terms if you think about it, is more than just a style; it is a sign of a certain orientation toward life and society. It is a kind of statement about oneself and one's philosophy. It reflects an essentially pastoral longing—for the simple life of shepherdesses and herdsmen in some simple and ideal society. In such a state one has escaped from history, from institutions, from complexity, and troubles, and one has attained a paradisical state.

This longing for an escape to nature has deep roots in the American experience. The Puritans came to America to establish a Holy Commonwealth in nature in the early 1600s and our writers and poets have celebrated our natural state for hundreds of years. Consider, for example, the concluding lines of Emerson's poem, "America, My Country," which was written in 1833:

> Land without history, land lying all
> In the plain daylight of the temperate zone,
>   Thy plain acts
> Without exaggeration done in day;
> Thy interests contested by their manifold
>   good sense,
> In their own clothes without the ornament
> Of bannered army harnessed in uniform.
> Land where—and 'tis in Europe counted a
>   reproach—
> Where man asks questions for which man was
>   made.
> A land without nobility, or wigs, or debt,
> No castles, no cathedrals, and no kings;
> Land of the forest.

These lines describe the philosophical stance implied by the natural look. What is stressed here? Such things as daylight, plain acts, no ornaments or uniforms (i.e., fancy clothes) and, of course, no wigs.

Whether Americans really are living in nature is beside the point; we have traditionally idealized it and used our alleged naturalness as a means of establishing an identity and as a way of reflecting our egalitarian and spiritual values. We see ourselves as living in nature and that is what is important, since people act on the basis of their perceptions of reality, not reality itself.

There is, I believe, a still deeper and more profound meaning to the natural look, American attitudes about naturalness, and our repudiation of Europe, history, and culture. This meaning has to do with the extension of the natural look to what might be called the natural state—the one that existed before the Fall. In the garden of Eden, Adam and Eve lived in a natural paradise and in a state of nudity. They had no knowledge of good and evil. It was only after they disobeyed God and ate from the tree of knowledge and *recognized that they were naked* that Adam and Eve were expelled from Paradise.

What Mircea Eliade writes, in *The Sacred and The Profane*, about baptismal nudity is relevant here:

> Baptismal nudity too bears a meaning that is at once ritual and metaphysical. It is abandoning "the old garment of corruption and sin, which the baptized person takes off in imitation of Christ, the garment with which Adam was

clothed after his sin"; but it is also return to primitive innocence, to Adam's state before the fall. "Oh admirable!" Cyril writes. "Ye were naked before the eyes of all and felt no shame. Because verily ye bear within you the image of the first Adam, who was naked in Paradise and felt no shame." (1961:134)

From this perspective, the natural look has a symbolic significance full of implications. On one level it is a kind of "antistyle" statement, a repudiation of "the made-up look" and all that goes with it. On another level, it is connected with American attitudes toward nature and attitudes connected with nature: egalitarianism, simplicity, honesty, individualism, and freedom. (This is contrasted to European decadence and sensuality, for example)

On a still deeper level, the natural look is connected with a desire to regain paradise and escape from guilt and shame. (I doubt that the person adopting the natural look is aware of the symbolic significance of the act. People seldom are aware of the full meaning or significance of what they do, wear, say, and so on.) This desire for paradise is, in itself, pregnant with meaning, for in paradise there is, Cyril tells us, "no shame." Eliade argues that movements like nudism reflect a "nostalgia" for Eden and are camouflaged or degenerated forms of religious behavior. Nudism and movements for complete sexual freedom represent, he says:

> the desire to re-establish the paradisical state before the Fall, when sin did not yet exist and there was no conflict between the pleasures of the flesh and conscience." (1961:207)

It would seem, then, that the natural look is a sign that suggests some kind of anxiety about guilt and sexuality, on the personal level—an anxiety that can be escaped by a return to natural paradise or, at the very least, a step in that direction.

Note: I realize there is also a natural look that involves makeup of a special kind—to give the effect of naturalness. I would imagine that the same dynamics and meaning apply to this natural look as well as to the no-makeup natural look.

Seventeen

Signs That Confound: Optical Illusions

Optical illusions may be described as special kinds of visual signs—signs that confuse and confound us by giving us "information" that poses problems for us. Take, for example, the optical illusion found below.

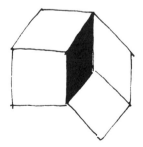

We find it difficult to interpret this drawing because the black, diamond-shaped area belongs simultaneously to two different cubes: it is the right-hand side of one cube *and* also the left-hand side of another cube. Our eye flits back and forth making either of two constructions but never one construction with both possibilties.

The phenomenon is strikingly similar to another puzzlement, the figure–ground representation below:

If we focus our attention on the white "figure" we see a vase; if we focus out attention on the black "ground," we see two profiles. But we cannot see both vase and profiles at the same time. It is this inability to see both figure and ground at the same time—or side and top in the illustration first discussed—that is at the heart of optical illusions.

What we have is a signifier that is jointly shared by either of two signifieds, so to speak. Our minds cannot deal with this kind of situation and we are forced to see the figure as either one thing or another. For a further example, consider the Levi's advertisement reproduced here. The eye finds it simply impossible to follow the lines which generate the three legs. There is too much information to digest and the information we have confuses us; the line which should be the top of the bottom leg has been appropriated by the middle leg.

We do not really have three legs, for as the following drawing shows, that would not confuse us (though the notion of a three-legged man is slightly bewildering). What we have in the Levi's advertisement is the illusion of three legs created by a line in the drawing functioning as the apparent top of the bottom leg and the apparent bottom of the middle trouser leg.

The three-legged pair of pants is a sign, all right—something that suggests the bizarre world of Charles Addams. But it is not an optical illusion.

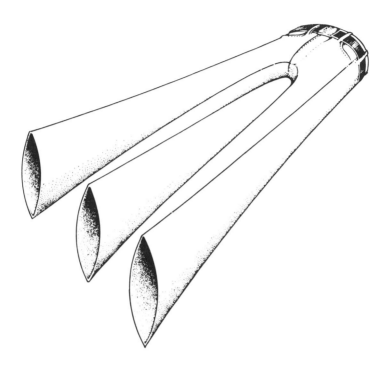

LEVI'S AND LEVI'S FOR GALS. PANTS MADE TO A DIFFERENT VISION.

Reprinted with permission of Levi Strauss & Co., San Francisco.

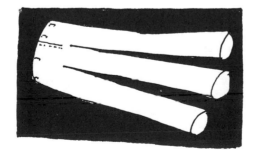

One of the things we learn from semiological analysis is that relationships are crucial in determining meaning. This insight is useful in understanding the work of the 16th-century fantastic painter, Arcimboldo.

ARCIMBOLDO

The paintings of Arcimboldo, the 16th-century "fantastic" painter, astonish us. Why? Because they are optical illusions that create images by using objects that have an identity in their own right, but which also look like something else. Thus his painting *Vertumnus* creates a man's face by assembling various fruits and vegetables. It is this double valence that is so arresting: a pear is obviously a pear—yet in the context of the painting it is also obviously a "man's" nose. From a distance it is the "gestalt," the image itself which dominates. It is when we get close and inspect the image that we notice it is really a collection of objects. It is a still life that is more than it seems.

What we learn from Arcimboldo's work is that *relationships* are crucial. In a given context—an assemblage in which a man's head and shoulders are being suggested—a pear is not just a pear but can also be a nose. Meaning comes from the system in which the items (objects, concepts) are embedded, and not from some kind of an identity things have on their own.

The tension between the claim of an object such as a pear for an identity of its own (a fruit one eats) and, at the same time, for a different one (a nose) is what creates the confusion and excitement. Arcimboldo is "fantastic" because he plays with our conception of reality and sense of the order of things.

What Arcimboldo achieves is an effect that has been described as "defamiliarization." As Victor Shklovsky, an important Russian aesthetician, has written:

Here is a work by Arcimboldo, a sixteenth-century Italian painter, who used various objects to create illusions of people.

> Habitualization devours objects, clothes, furniture, one's wife, and the fear of war. "If all the complex lives of many people go on unconsciously, then such lives are as if they had never been."
>
> Art exists to help us recover the sensation of life; it exists to make us feel things, to make the stone *stony*. The end of art is to give a sensation of the object as seen, not as recognized. The technique of art is to make things "unfamiliar," to make forms obscure, so as to increase the difficulty and the duration of perception. *In art, it is our experience of the process of construction that counts, not the finished product.* (Quoted in Scholes, 1974:83–84)

Arcimboldo forces us to create a face out of pears and flowers. He does not give us the face to peruse. We thus become intimately involved in the process of creation (or perhaps re-creation). And we regain a sense of wonder and awe about the human face.

Arcimboldo pushes things to extremes. We cannot say of the hero of this painting "He's got a nose like a pear." The simile is too weak. We must use metaphor, pure and simple. "The hero of this painting has a nose that is a pear, a pear nose." But in the context of the painting, of course, the pear functions as a nose.

There is something marvelously comic about all this; you can sense that Arcimboldo is playing with us. It is something like the riddles we used to ask one another: "When is a _____ not a _____?" "When is a door not a door?" "When it's ajar." Arcimboldo asks us, "When is an eyebrow not an eyebrow?" His answer is, "When it is a peapod." Verbally it doesn't make much sense; visually it is quite comic.

What fantastic artists like Arcimboldo (and other artists who do "bizarre" work) force us to recognize is that our perception of reality is always tentative; there is always a gap between appearance and reality even though we may not be aware of it. In Arcimboldo's paintings we can see this gap (though under the correct circumstances we may be taken in) but in other styles and genres we may be fooled much more easily. Thus fantastic art like Arcimboldo's functions, ironically, to force us all to be more careful about our sense of reality.

Eighteen

Sign Modifiers

I have suggested earlier that signs (or, more precisely, complex signs) stand between the sign element or signeme and icons (in which we have a large number of signs). Because of this, signs are sometimes difficult to see or understand. There are problems of clutter and competition to be considered in addition to other difficulties. To offset many of these problems, those who use signs often modify them in various ways—which is what I will consider here. In the chart that follows, I list some ways of modifying signs and explain how these modifications function.

Modification	Techniques Used	Result
Intensifier	Repetition, Size, Color, etc.	Elements Made Stronger
Focuser	White Space, Design Vectors	Attention
Duplicator	Different Kinds of Signs	Redundancy
Clarifier	Establishment of Context	Meaning, Lower Ambiguity
Minimizer	Clutter, Mimic Context	Camouflage

Consider, for example, the typewritten page as a system of signs and the typewriter as a sign generator (which it is, par excellence). In addition to the words one can type on a typewriter, there are various design strategies one can use for various purposes. Thus, one can underline a word to call attention to it or type it in all caps or both underline it and type it in all caps. One can stretch a word out by typing spaces between the letters. One can also single-space material; this is a convention for quoted material though it is used for other purposes as well. One can use space to focus attention on a word—a word isolated from all others stands out.

Let's look at some of these visual display strategies now.

Sign.

Sign.

S I G N.   S I G N.   S-I-G-N.

SIGN.

One can also single-space material; this is a convention for quoted material, though it is used for other purposes as well.

The typewriter may not be a powerful device for manipulating signs but it does have a certain amount of capacity. I've not said anything about typewriter faces or the "look" one gets with an expensive electronic typewriter, but these matters are also signs and convey much information.

Now I would like to turn to the matter of sign duplication and consider the matter of bathroom signs. In a unisexual society (or one much less squeamish than ours) there would be no gender signs on bathroom doors. The fact that we use any signs on bathroom doors indicating gender is, itself, a sign which tells us soemthing about our sexual attitudes, notions of propriety, and anxieties about urinating and defecating.

If one is to put a sign on a bathroom door there are, it seems, three possibilities: one can use a linguistic sign, an icon, or a symbol to distinguish male from female bathrooms. The chart below demonstrates this.

Bathroom Signs

Men	Women		
		Linguistic Sign	Must be able to read language.
		Iconic Sign	Must be able to see resemblance between sign and objects.
♂	♀	Symbol	Must know conventions behind symbols.

Obviously the iconic sign, if the figures are portrayed simply and unambig-uously, is the easiest for most people to interpret. Often linguistic and iconic signs are used to reinforce one another in cases where there may be confusion or problems—as in international airports, for instance.

All of this presupposes, of course, that a person recognizes that a room is a bathroom. This is seldom rendered only iconically. But since bathrooms are usually the only rooms that are identified by sex, by a process of deduction people recognize bathrooms for what they are.

When we wish to "focus" attention on a sign, two of the more important techniques are using white space to "isolate" the sign and force one to consider it, and using design vectors to lead the eye to the sign. We are dealing here with composition or design elements, which play an important role in generating "display" or its opposite, camouflage. Size is not a crucial matter; a large object in the midst of many other objects can get lost in the clutter. What is important is contrast...and white space.

I mentioned, also, that signs often need clarification; this is done by establishing contexts. Thus a hypodermic needle means "health" in the context of a hospital and "drug abuse" in a dimly lit room or an alley. Heavy breathing means passion in the bedroom, perversion on the telephone (when accompanied by other signs or absent signs, that is), and exercise in a gymnasium.

Various modification techniques are necessary because we use signs in so many different ways for so many different purposes. At times we wish to make ourselves clear and at other times to be ambiguous and unclear. Sometimes we want to emphasize something or make a point by saying the same thing in different ways. Therefore, we use the various sign modifiers at our disposal, often with questionable results.

I am a cartoonist and have been drawing illustrations for magazines and books for a number of years. It was only after I had read the semiologists that I understood what I was doing when I drew cartoons—searching for visual signifiers that would suggest, to my readers, specific signifieds. And finding signifiers that do so with a certain element of humor and absurdity.

CARTOONING*

Every three months I get a large manilla envelope in the mail. It is from the editors of *The Journal of Communication* and contains xeroxes of the first pages of articles that will be appearing in the next issue. My job is to draw funny illustrations—cartoons which, it is hoped, will brighten up the pages of the magazine and, at the same time, suggest something about the subject and article.

I read the pages over carefully, looking, often almost desperately, for something to hang a drawing on. Some articles are rather abstract and I find it difficult (and at times impossible) to think of anything suitable. As I read the articles I jot ideas down in the margins. Then I take my pen in hand and start drawing.

It really is a lot of fun, though it is often frustrating. I have a particular style of drawing, a certain kind of line, and I work under certain limitations. I do not, as a rule, do gag cartoons with words. So everything has to be expressed pictorially. My tools are a fountain pen, a black felt nib pen and a sense of humor.

Note: A modified form of this essay appeared in *The Public Communication Review*, Volume 1, 1981. Reprinted with permission.

My biggest problem involves ideas. "What can I draw," I keep asking myself, "that will mean 'moral violation in soap operas' or 'the information society'" (or any one of a number of other subjects). The game is to find something understandable but not too obvious, and it often takes a lot of thought and playing around to do so. What I really do, in the final analysis, is search for signifiers. *Cartoons, from this point of view, are complex sign systems which generate meaning by using a vast collection of signifying elements that readers can interpret fairly easily.*

This definition is not too different from the standard definitions of cartoons we find in dictionaries. Thus, according to *The Random House Dictionary of the English Language* (the unabridged edition) a cartoon is a "sketch or drawing, usually humorous, as in a newspaper or periodical, symbolizing, satirizing, or caricaturing some action, subject, or person of popular interest." (Cartoons do not have continuing characters or dialogue in balloons like comic strips and comic books.)

Political cartoonists make great use of caricatures while social cartoonists (such as the people we find in *The New Yorker*, for example) tend to use stereotyped figures who represent various kinds of people, occupations, and social types, which can be caricatured and ridiculed. These definitions and descriptions do not do justice to the power of the cartoon. Many people consider cartoons trivial because they are funny and are not an elevated art form. This kind of thinking underestimates the power of cartoons to chronicle our madnesses, make our thoughts concrete, and communicate certain ideas that other forms of communication find difficult to do.

As a cartoonist I can exaggerate a movement, I can simplify and focus attention on something, I can suggest motion, emotion—there are all kinds of effects that can be achieved with the cartoon. Recently, for example, a

Headlines.

colleague came to me with a problem. He had written a very successful text on announcing and performance and wanted me to do some cartoons of the signs used in radio and television stations to indicate commercial breaks, the need to get closer to a microphone, and so on. He had tried taking photographs of people but found that the photographs were too busy and didn't have enough display.

I was able to get rid of clutter and focus attention on a particular sign and, by giving the characters doing the signing funny faces, for example, I was also able to inject some humor into what ordinarily would have been a rather dull and visually messy situation. Although cartoons may not be elevated art forms and although the average person does little more than glance at most cartoons, they should not be dismissed lightly. Cartoons have affected our language (and given us the term "gerrymander"), cartoons have destroyed politicians (Nast's brilliant cartoons about Boss Tweed would be the classic example), cartoons have ridiculed some of our most absurd fads and fashions, cartoons have given us political symbology (the Democratic donkey and the Republican elephant) and cartoons, almost always, have provided us with laughs. No small thing.

Cartoons function by providing us with resonant images which both reflect and affect our social and political order. And all they ask of us is a momentary glance and, perhaps, a chuckle. Since every laugh is also a lesson, the cartoon teaches us as it entertains us. What other art form can you think of that asks so little and does so much?

Nineteen

Manifest and Latent Meanings in Signs

From our discussion of signs to this point it is quite obvious that signs are complex phenomena and demand careful and considered "readings." Here I would like to focus on an aspect of signs that has been alluded to but not detailed—the fact that signs have latent as well as manifest meanings and functions. The following chart defines and contrasts "manifest" and "latent" and explains how these concepts have generally been used.

Manifest	Meaning is obvious	Interpretation intended
Latent	Meaning is hidden	Interpretation not intended

The manifest meaning of a sign will be considered to be the one which is that meaning which is obvious and the intended result desired by the maker of the sign. It is, we might say, perfectly clear and purposefully so. A traffic signs saying "STOP" would be a good example of this—to the extent, I must caution, that any sign is ever perfectly clear.

The latent meaning of a sign from our perspective is neither intended nor obvious; it is buried in the sign and in the unconscious of the maker of the sign and the viewer. It has been suggested by some that the goal of sociology is to uncover the latent functions of phenomena—thereby making them manifest and obvious to all involved. This leads to what has been described as the "paradox of sociological knowledge," for if it is the case that society is held together by the latent functions of phenomena, the more we know the worse off we are.

Photograph by Jan Browman

Cocktail sign.

Our rule, then, as far as signs are concerned—particularly visual signs—is "there's generally more than meets the eye." As an example let us consider the neon signs one often sees in front of bars which show a martini glass and a swizzle stick inside it. A representation of this sign is shown here.

The manifest meaning of this sign is rather obvious—it is an iconic representation of a drink and a swizzle stick. The latent meaning, I would like to suggest, is much more interesting, What we have, from this perspective, is highly erotic and sexual: we find a phallus pointing at a woman's vagina. We see this when I supply a couple of lines to the original drawing or sign:

The neon sign suggests (and we are not conscious of this, I surmise) male and female sexual relations and this notion is reinforced by a word one often sees accompanying this sign, "cocktails." "Cock" is a slang term for the penis and "tail" for women. Thus—on the latent level—the word cocktail is loaded, sexually. Logically one would expect to see such signs outside of "body bars," where men and women pick each other up for sexual dalliances and alliances—usually of a very temporary nature.

Thus, not only is a sign something that can be made to stand for something else, but it is also something that often stands for things we aren't even aware of but which, I believe, affect us profoundly. Let me offer another example here—the video game (and craze) "Pac Man." We can find in "Pac Man," I believe, a sign that a rather profound change is taking place in the American psyche. Earlier video games (and the video-game phenomenon is significant in its own right) such as "Space Invaders" and so on, involved rocket ships coursing through outer space, blasting aliens and hostile forces with ray guns, lazer beams, and other weapons, and represented a very different orientation from "Pac Man." The games were highly phallic and they also expressed a sense of freedom and openness. The games were played in outer space and one had a sense of infinite possibility.

"Pac Man," however, represents something quite different. The game takes place in a labyrinth which implies, metaphorically, that we are all trapped, closeted in a claustrophobic situation in which the nature of things is that we must either eat or be eaten. This oral aspect of the game suggests further that there is some kind of a diffuse regression taking place and we

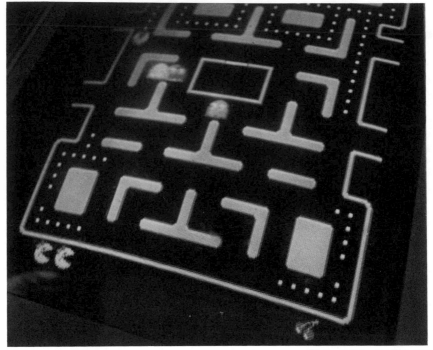

Photograph by Jan Browman

Pac-Man board.

have moved from the phallic stage (guns, rockets) to the oral stage (eating, biting).

Regression often takes place in people as a means of coping with anxiety and there is good reason to suspect that the popularity of a game like "Pac Man" indicates that our young people, who play the game, are coping with their anxieties by regressing (in the service of their egos). This may be because they are, for some reason, now afraid of taking on responsibilities and feel anxious about long-term relationships and mature interpersonal sexuality. When we regress to more child-like stages we escape from the demands of adulthood—but we pay a considerable price.

It is these aspects of "Pac Man" that disturb me. On the surface it is just a game. But the nature of the game—its design, which suggests that we are all prisoners of a system from which there is no escape, and its regressive aspects—must give all who speculate about the hidden meanings in phenomena something to think about.

Robinson Crusoe is not just the hero of an important book: he is, in addition, a model (paradigmatic) hero who reflects important attitudes toward the world and society. He is a "mythic" hero who was the prototype for the American pioneer and, in turn, many American values that still influence people in various ways.

ROBINSON CRUSOE AND THE MYTH OF THE SELF-MADE MAN

Robinson Crusoe, the hero of Defoe's great book, is one of the supreme paradigmatic heroes in Western literature and a character whose influence is much greater than it might seem. We underestimate the importance of the book when we classify it as merely a children's book, full of exciting adventures, and let it go at that. It is much better to consider the book, its characters, their values, and the influence of these on future generations.

In *Myths, Dreams and Mysteries*, Mircea Eliade explains the way heroes function:

> Concurrently with official pedagogy, and long after this has ceased to exert its authority, modern man is subjected to the influence of a potent if diffuse mythology that offers him a number of patterns for imitation. Heroes, real and imaginary, play an important part in the formation of...adolescents: the characters in tales of adventure, heroes of war, screen favorites, etc. This mythology is continually enriched with the growing years; we meet, one after another, the exemplary figures thrown up by changes of fashion, and we try to become like them. (1967:33)

These mythic heroes and heroines are models, paradigmatic figures with whom we identity and whom we imitate in various ways.

I use the term "myth" here to suggest pattern or charter, not "error" or mistaken belief. Myths play important roles in cultures; they are sacred histories that help determine the values, beliefs, and actions of people—even if those who are influenced by them are not aware that this is the case. People are not aware of these myths because they are often camouflaged and secularized and the mythic heroes and heroines are found not in religious tracts alone but also in novels, plays, and most recently in popular culture. This notion is by no means held only by Eliade. Much scholarship has focused on the relationship that exists between myths and behavior. Thus we have a book such as Raphael Patai's *Myth and Modern Man* which describes itself on its cover as "A new understanding of our times through an analysis of unsuspected mythic motivations in our values, goals, choices, illusions, fears, and anxieties." With this perspective on the role of myths and heroes in mind, let us consider *Robinson Crusoe*.

In a masterly essay on the book, "Robinson Crusoe as a Myth," Ian Watt writes (in Robert N. Wilson, ed. *The Arts in Society*):

> It is easy to see that Robinson Crusoe is related to three essential themes of modern civilization—which we can briefly designate as "Back to Nature," "The Dignity of Labor," and "Economic Man." Robinson Crusoe seems to have become a kind of culture hero representing all three of these related but not wholly congruent ideas. It is true that if we examine what Defoe actually wrote and what he may be thought to have intended, it appears that *Robinson Crusoe* hardly supports some of the symbolic uses to which the pressure of the needs of our society has made it serve. But this, of course, is in keeping with the status of *Robinson Crusoe* as a myth, for we learn as much from the varied shapes that a myth takes in men's minds as from the form in which it first arose. It is not an author but society that metamorphoses a story into a myth, by retaining only what its unconscious needs dictate and forgetting everything else. (1964:152)

We will consider some of these points in our analysis of the book.

Robinson Crusoe appeared in 1719, well after the American "experiment" had begun, but it is an excellent example of the world view that sustained the American pioneer and was to inform much of American social thought, and does to this day. Cast ashore on an uninhabited tropical island, Crusoe spends 28 years domesticating it, making it capable of supporting him; all the while, with nobody to talk to, he is, by force of circumstance, a prisoner of psychology. Crusoe seems to be a model of self-sufficiency. By virtue of heroic labors he builds stockades, domesticates animals, makes a comfortable home for himself, and survives much better than one might expect.

However, he is lucky. He has all kinds of tools and other implements which he takes from the wreckage of the ship that he was aboard. In a sense he is a perfect model for the pioneer. Thanks to God's mercy he is carried to an uninhabited territory which he then can transform, due to his native intelligence, willingness to work hard, and knowledge. He not only has the advantage of some tools of civilization, namely the gun, but also carpenter's tools and other such commodities.

He is then to spend more than 25 years *by himself*; in the process of making his way he offers the equivalent of "a meditation" on the nature of life: a monologue lasting almost 30 years—with only a parrot to talk with. We must also notice that to his good fortune nature is bountiful. He finds excellent water supplies, all kinds of animals to eat, and other foods such as fruits and vegetables. Yet nature cannot be left to itself! He must impose some kind of order on it, build stockades, gardens, and dwellings; he then becomes, as he puts it, a king. He transforms the wilderness into a more manageable state and the "Island of Despair" becomes, instead, a kind of paradise:

> How mercifully can our great Creator treat his creatures, even in those conditions in which they seemed to be overwhelmed in destruction! How can he sweeten the bitterest providences, and give us cause to praise him for dungeons and prisons! What a table was here spread for me in a wilderness, where I saw nothing at first but to perish for hunger!

> It would have made a stoic smile, to have seen me and my little family sit down to dinner: there was my majesty, the prince and lord of the whole island! I had the lives of all my subjects at absolute command; I could hang, draw, give liberty, and take it away, and no rebels among all my subjects.

> Then to see how like a king I dine, too, all alone.... (Defoe, 1946:218)

Robinson Crusoe can be a king (of nature) and live well enough to make a stoic smile because he has the correct solution to the problem of how one leads the good life: *in nature* but not as a natural man. The natural men are the cannibals, who feast on human flesh. They are as bad, in their state of savagery, as men at the other extreme, the world of society, where they can plan to make fortunes on the slave trade, It was this which lured Crusoe from his plantation in Brazil and led to his being cast on the island. He had been prospering in Brazil but "fell in" with some people planning to engage in the slave trade and sailed from Brazil on his ill-fated voyage. We might think of Crusoe's 28 years on the island as a penance he had to endure to atone for his evil intentions. He who would have enslaved others becomes enslaved himself—to himself.

It is Crusoe's mission to bring order to the wilderness, or, in terms of a distinction made in Ward's *Jackson: Symbol for an Age*, to transform wilderness into nature. The table was spread for him in the wilderness but

Crusoe, being a creature of society, cannot accept the wilderness and live according to its canons. When his linen clothes wear out, he does not go naked, even though the weather was so hot he didn't need them:

> and though it was true, that the weather was so violent hot that there was no need for clothes, yet I could not go quite naked: no, though I had been inclined to it, which I was not; nor could I abide the thoughts of it, though I was all alone. (Defoe, 1946:196)

Instead Crusoe makes a suit of furs (and a fur umbrella to shield him from the hot sun). He has moved from civilization closer to nature, but he has *not* gone native.

It is not much of a jump from Crusoe, dressed in his fur skins, bringing order to the wilderness of the "Island of Despair," to the pioneer, in fur skins, conquering the American forest. Both are prisoners of psychology in that both live beyond society, though they carry elements of it with them, and are forced, therefore, to create themselves. Crusoe is an archetype of the self-reliant individual and as such, serves as a model for the American pioneer and the contemporary American trying to live his or her "American Dream." Crusoe demonstrates that you do not need society in order to have a good life, though a few of the "tools" of civilization are a help.

He must battle cannibals and pirates, monsters of nature and civilization, but he can overwhelm them and live "the good life"—one good enough to make a stoic smile. Since I have been using the discipline of psychology as a means toward understanding the reasons for American individualism, we might take one of its theories to explain the self-confidence the Crusoe-inspired person has in his or her abilities. It might be an example of what is called "infantile omnipotence," the belief (supposedly) in the heads of newly born infants, that they *are* the world and have it "in absolute command." Everything reduces itself to will-power, the supreme psychological category as far as Americans are concerned. It is will-power which leads to creation, rather than "going native" and just existing on the bounties of the wilderness.

Robinson Crusoe is a story of a man who spends 25 years alone, with no society to corrupt him, but he has already been corrupted. He will do his penance and transform the wilderness and when he has done this he can return to society. Even on his island he could not escape from evil, for if man in society is evil, he is also evil in a state of nature. The pirate and the cannibal, that is, the social criminal and the natural criminal, show that evil pervades human life. If you try to escape the social criminal and run away to a desert island, somewhere, the natural criminal will be waiting—to devour you. Robinson Crusoe is apolitical. You need to have several people in order to have politics. Since, to a great extent, people base their political philosophy upon a view of the world which says that man is, innately, good or evil, it is important for us to understand this matter. Crusoe may have been corrupted by society and he may have encountered cannibals, but does this mean that all men living in society *must* be corrupted or that all men living in nature *must* be evil?

Twenty

Analyzing Signs and Sign Systems

I would like to offer a check-list for analyzing photographs, advertisements, and frames from films in addition to less complicated signs. I am concerned with the various kinds of signs being used, how they generate meaning, how they relate to one another, what they reflect about our society and culture, and the problems they pose for the semiologist or other "interpreters" of signs.

Let us assume we are dealing with an advertisement in a magazine. We should be concerned with some or all of the following matters:

A. What is the general ambience of the advertisement? What mood does it create? How does it do this?

B. What is the design of the advertisement? Does it use axial balance or some other form? How are the basic components or elements of the advertisement arranged?

C. What is the relationship that exists between pictorial elements and written material and what does this tell us?

D. What is the spatiality in the advertisement? Is there a lot of "white space" or is the advertisement full of graphic and written elements (that is, "busy")?

Fidji: le parfum
des paradis retrouvés.

<u>Fid</u>ji de Guy Laroche.

De la Haute Couture à la Haute Parfumerie

This advertisement for Fidgi perfume is full of interesting signs, symbols, and significance. And sex.

E. What signs and symbols do we find? What role do the various signs and symbols play in the advertisement?

F. If there are figures (men, women, children, animals) in the advertisement, what are they like? What can be said about their facial expressions, poses, hairstyle, age, sex, hair color, ethnicity, education, occupation, relationships (of one to the other), and so on?

G. What does the background tell us? Where is the action in the advertisement taking place and what significance does this background have?

H. What action is taking place in the advertisement and what significance does this action have? (This might be described as the plot of the advertisement.)

I. What theme or themes do we find in the advertisement? What is the advertisement about? (The plot of an advertisement may involve a man and a woman drinking but the theme might be jealousy, faithlessness, ambition, passion, etc.)

J. What about the language used in the advertisement? Does it essentially provide information or generate some kind of an emotional response? Or both? What techniques are used by the copywriter: humor, alliteration, "definitions" of life, comparisons, sexual innuendo, and so on?

K. What typefaces are used and what impressions do these typefaces convey?

L. What is the item being advertised and what role does it play in American culture and society?

M. What about aesthetic decisions? If the advertisement is a photograph, what kind of a shot is it? What significance do long shots, medium shots, close-ups have? What about the lighting, use of color, angle of the shot?

N. What sociological, political, economic or cultural attitudes are indirectly reflected in the advertisement? An advertisement may be about a pair of blue jeans but it might, indirectly, reflect such matters as sexism, alienation, stereotyped thinking, conformism, generational conflict, loneliness, elitism, and so on.

Each word in the famous "Reach Out And Touch Someone" campaign is analyzed here to show what these commercials and advertisements reflect about American culture and society.

(RO)²ATS: REACH OUT, REACH OUT AND TOUCH SOMEONE

The "Reach Out" commercials of Bell Telephone have attained the status of being "classics" and there are few people in American society who have not been exposed to one or more of these ads. The making of one 30-second commercial for this series has been described in Michael Arlen's captivating book, *Thirty Seconds*. It shows the amount of thought, hard work, and craziness involved in the advertising business, in general, and the making of commercials, in particular.

In this section, I will concern myself only with the five words in the campaign—reach out and touch someone—and I will deal with the significance of those words for the American psyche and American culture. Arlen has shown how complicated it was to make one 30-second commercial for this campaign. I would like to show how much there is in the five-word theme line.

1. ***Reach.*** In the context of phoning, we use the word "reach" to mean we've established contact with someone, that we've made some kind of a connection. Reach also has something to do with extending our sphere of influence and, indirectly, our power to influence events and people. We also talk about "reaching" a person in the sense of getting on the same "wave length," penetrating barriers, and establishing some sort of intellectual or emotional (or both) rapport.

Reaching is an activity, it is something one does. The reaching (out) that AT&T wants us to do is also an activity: making long-distance phone calls, overcoming the resistance many people have (and fear they have) of doing this. There is a power involved in reaching others. They can be summoned, no matter where they are; after all, who can hear a phone ring and not answer it? So, there is an element of coercion here that must be considered.

The need to reach is something else to think about. If one needs to reach, one is separated, apart from, distant (as in long-distance) from another, who one wants to reach. In this sense, reach is a sign of the alienation that is so powerful in our society. Our families are all split up nowadays, people move from job to job every few years (or at least they used to) and all that keeps families and friends in contact, aside from letters, is the telephone. (That's what "tele" means—distance.) The phone annihilates distance, if only for a while, just as the sound of another's voice helps assuage our loneliness and feeling of separation.

2. **Out.**   "Out" is the opposite of in, so when one reaches out, there is an implicit assumption that one is in (as "in the center of") and is communicating with people who are on some periphery. They are "out of it," or, existentially speaking, in the middle of nowhere. "Everyone believes," a wit once said, "that the world revolves around his or her backyard."

There is something questionable about being "out"—it seems as if one lacks taste, the correct values, discrimation, and so on. Being "out" is very close to being "out of it," so that when we reach out, we are really doing a kind of favor to the lost souls we contact by the phone. Of course sometimes we call people and they are out literally, and that is infuriating, since we feel our power is being challenged. The worst form of being out, here, is when we are told the party we are seeking is "in conference," which means our outreach is being rejected (generally) by someone who does not want us to reach out to him or her.

3. **And.**   "And" is pure functionality. When we reach out, so the "and" tells us, something will happen. There is a consequence promised, one that will please us. "And" is a connective; it joins things just as the phone call "joins" people. "And" is a phone connection in the context of this commercial.

4. **Touch.**   What a wonderful word for the phone company; it couldn't have found a more resonant word, one that means so many different things—all of which are good. At the figurative level, "touch" means to have an emotional impact on someone. Touch implies affect, affection, feeling. The purpose of our reaching out, it is suggested, is to enable us to "touch" someone; if not physically (with a hug or a kiss) then psychologically, by the sound of our voice.

There is an implied metaphor here. "Phoning is being there" in the sense that one's presence, one's voice, can substitute for one's body. Sound destroys distance...and the sound of one's voice is the next best thing to being there. (Actually it may even be better, for one can always hang up after a talk with someone and "escape." If you're there, sometimes you find yourself a captive.) This aspect of touching must not be underestimated. There is a side of touching that suggests temporality, briefness as in "touching bases" or "getting in touch" for a short bit of information exchange.

The aspect of touch that the phone company is concerned with, from a technical point of view, is the touch-tone phone, which costs more to rent than the traditional mechanical dial phone. Thus, in the best of all possible worlds for the phone company, one uses the touch-tone phone to get in touch with everybody one wants to. And the more people the better. This leads us to our next consideration.

5. *Someone.*   The commercials always show someone being "reached" by the phone. Little old ladies, grandpa, cute kids, etc. The someone who is called, after all, has to be "reached" emotionally (which implies some kind of prior relationship). There is something ironic about the word. It is an impersonal word but is meant to be personal; "someone" is almost as vague as "anyone," though "someone" is used here to mean someone in particular.

There is an element of anonymity connected with the word "someone," and a hint of desperation. This, also, stems from alienation and estrangement. At times, in the depths of loneliness, one wants only to be able to reach someone—maybe even anyone? Our society makes us feel we need to reach someone, anyone, at times. And the phone makes it possible.

6. *Conclusions.*   "Reach Out, Reach Out and Touch Someone" is, whatever else it might be, a command. We are told twice to "reach out" and though this command may be jazzy and catchy, it is still a command. The rhythm and clever way in which the song is sung (often with an interesting use of syncopation in the first "re–each") may mask the imperative nature of the lyrics, but they are bald commands. "Reach out!"

This is necessary, the phone company believes, because people must be coerced—even if the coercion is cleverly done—into making more long-distance phone calls. Not making long-distance phone calls becomes, and this is implicit in the commercials, a sign of one's selfishness and self-centeredness, an indicator that one doesn't *want* to "reach" people (and give them the gift of love). *Not phoning thus becomes a sign of dereliction of duty, of abandonment, of a hard heart.* Not phoning is a sin of omission which the phone company finds repugnant. It is, we are led to believe, the eighth deadly sin.

Thus, beneath the good humor of "the girls" (all of whom are 70 or so) "hitting it," which we find in one of the more memorable commercials in this series, is a subtle element of coercion. And of distortion. This distortion comes from the routinization or naturalization of behavior that is somewhat unusual. Making long-distance phone calls is posited, in these commercials, as the kind of activity that one is expected to do (in much the same way that offering sexual favors to all who demand them is posited as natural and normal in the *Playboy* world-view). If you don't reach out (or put out) there's something wrong with *you*! Being afraid or not wishing to make long-distance phone calls all the time, we are led to believe, is old-fashioned; it is a prejudice we would be well to rid ourselves of. I have no fault to find with people making phone calls—what bothers me is that people are subjected, in the guise of humorous and "warm" commercials, to subtle and insidious manipulation, to hidden compulsions that attack their reason and autonomy.

This analysis has proceded, I imagine, along lines that both AT&T and N. W. Ayer, would probably find absurd. "Just some simple commercials," they would argue, "meant to entertain people and get them to make long-distance phone calls." Would that it were so simple. If it took almost a million dollars, six months, and more than ten thousand feet of film to get the 45 feet necessary for *one* 30-second television commercial, I would say there's more than meets the eye in the "Reach Out" campaign. And it might not be a good idea to wonder where we got the *urge* when we reach out for the phone to "reach out and touch someone."

Twenty-one

Codes

One of the most common complaints among my students (and many other young people with whom I come into contact) about the situation in which they find themselves is that they are being "programmed." By this they mean that their parents (who have certain goals in mind for them) and the social ambience in which the young people have grown up is very *directive*. Usually the direction is upward, as in "upward mobility." Since most people in America are middle class or below, they all can see a level toward which they aspire—or think they should aspire—or toward which they think their children should aspire.

In America, where we have a myth of absolute freedom (the so-called self-made man) and believe that freedom involves an escape from history and society and tradition, we rebel against all of this, in the name of rebelling against "programming." But where do we turn? Inevitably, alas, to other "programs," other "traditions," other ways of organizing our lives. Certainly we must organize our lives in *some* way. We have to eat, sleep, go to the toilet, see a doctor every once in a while, and take care of other needs—some natural and others social. Some people just "fall apart," but this, too, is a kind of "program" or reverse program—and it involves certain ways of behaving that are just as rigid, in a sense, as in a typical middle class, upwardly mobile American.

When people talk about being "programmed," then, it is not so much that they resent "programs" but that they resent having *certain* "programs" inflicted on them. What they want is a choice of "programs" or some kind of a "program" that allows self-determination, freedom, choice, openness—a program that is not restrictive and does not intrude upon them. This may be an "impossible dream," beyond the capacity of any of our computer designers or programmers, but it is an ideal that is very much in people's minds. Now it may be that some degree of randomness is a part of every "program" or can be designed into societies, so this dream of freedom and autonomy is more nearly attainable. I do not know whether it is possible, or where the line between an open-ended nonintrusive "program" ends and chaos begins.

But it certainly seems possible to "open people's eyes" to the extent to which programming goes on so that on the personal or individual level, people can decide which "programs" they wish to adopt for themselves—assuming that some combination of "programs" is necessary. We have to have certain "programs" in mind which we call habit and choice—otherwise we would have to spend every other waking minute trying to decide what to do and how to do it.

There is, I think, a better way of dealing with this problem of "being programmed" and that is to use a slightly different concept—what I call *culture-codes*. "Programming" is too one-sided and simplistic; it assumes a passive subject (the person as computer) ready to do the bidding of the "programmer"; instead we find people are not as passive as computers and cannot (we all pray) be "programmed" as simply and completely as computers. The fear that they can is the subject of countless science-fiction stories and dystopias.

I like the term *culture-codes* because it calls our attention to the fact that culture (and there are countless definitions of the term) is a "programmer," and is directive. In other words, culture can be thought of as a collection of codes which shapes people's behavior, to varying degrees and in various ways, depending upon the circumstances. There are two meanings to the term "code": first, codes refer to systematic bodies of statutes, rules, and so on, as in the Napoleonic Code or the Code of Hammurabi. The second meaning of code involves the idea of something secret—a set of figures or letters or symbols with arbitrary meanings, but which can be deciphered if you know the principle of organization of the code. If you don't know this, you must "break" the code—that is, find it.

If we combine the two aspects of codes—the fact that they are systematic and secret—we arrive at what I call *culture-codes*. *Culture-codes are*: (1) *directives in our culture which we do not recognize (generally) but* (2) *which have a highly articulated structure and which are very specific.* I prefer to use the term *culture-code* instead of culture because of all the problems connected with the word "culture"; some think of it as certain kinds of art, what is often called "high culture" or "elite" culture. Others (the anthropologists) use it for everything not natural that is passed on from one generation to the next. But this meaning of culture does not adequately suggest its directive quality, which is why I prefer *culture-codes*. *Culture-codes, then, are secret structures which shape our behavior*...or at least frequently influence it.

The revelation of such structures is the key to the fascination Sherlock Holmes has for people. Let us turn to *A Study in Scarlet* for an example. Dr. Watson, Holmes' companion and confidant, is telling the reader about Holmes and mentions an article:

> Its somewhat ambitious title was *The Book of Life*, and it attempted to show how much an observant man might learn by an accurate and systematic examination of all that came in his way. It struck me as being a remarkable mixture of shrewdness and of absurdity. The reasoning was close and intense, but the deductions appeared to me to be far-fetched and exaggerated....

> "From a drop of water," said the writer, "a logician could infer the possibility of an Atlantic or a Niagara without having seen or heard of one or the other. *So all life is a great chain, the nature of which is known whenever we are shown a single link of it.*" (1969:159) [My italics]

Holmes can "read structure"; because he has a fine memory and keen powers of observation, he is able to deduce all kinds of things to astonish Watson and foil criminals. "Elementary, my dear Watson," he says—and he is correct. By being able to put elements into relation with one another he is able to solve puzzles; and when he explains his "train of reasoning" to us, it is all so simple that we always wonder why *we* didn't see it in the first place.

I'm not certain that life is a great chain, as Holmes thought it was, but it does seem that human behavior, society, and probably the universe are structured—and we can penetrate what frequently *seems* irrational and chaotic and find order and structure. What we have to look for to understand man better, then, are *culture-codes*. They are the keys to understanding behavior, to seeing beneath the apparent randomness of things and obtaining insights into what motivates people.

One of the problems we face in dealing with codes stems from the fact that they can operate at different levels—often at many different levels at the same time. Think of humor, for example. Some humor is universal; here I'm thinking of the antics of clowns and mimes which almost anyone can understand or at least appreciate. Other humor seems to be national, or, in other words, deeply affected by matters connected with nations, their histories and identities. Some examples are English understatement, American exuberance and overstatement (tall tales, etc.) and so on.

Then, within nations, there are other subcategories such as regional humor (Yankee, Southern), local humor (Bostonian) and individual humor (a given person's sense of humor). In the chart that follows I've categorized the levels of humor, offered explanations of what causes them, and given examples.

Code Levels

Level	Explanation	Example
Universal	Nature	Mimes
National	History	American Characters, e.g. Huck Finn
Regional	Geography	Country Bumpkin vs. City Slicker
Local	Groups	Jokes about gays in San Francisco
Individual	Personality	Jokes I like

The fact that different code levels exist means that there can be a great deal of confusion. For instance, the sender of a message can be operating at one level but the receiver of the message operating at another. In addition, factors such as educational level, ethnicity, social class, and race play a role and further complicate communication.

There is also the matter of kinds of codes. It has been suggested by the French semiologist Pierre Guiraud, in his book, *Semiology*, that there are three important kinds of codes: social codes, aesthetic codes, and logical codes.

The attributes and characteristics of these codes are found in the following chart.

Kinds of Codes

Social Codes	Aesthetic Codes	Logical Codes
Relations Among Men and Women in Society	Interpreting and Evaluating Arts and Literature	Understanding Nature and the World
Identity	Art	Highway Code
Rank	Literature	Symbolic Logic
Manners	Theatre	Braille
Fashion	Comic Strips	Morse Code
Rituals	Westerns	Sign Language
Greetings	Folk Tales	Sephamores
Games	Soap Operas	Zodiac Signs

Form **990-PF**
Department of the Treasury
Internal Revenue Service

Return of Private Foundation
Exempt from Income Tax
Under Section 501(c)(3) of the Internal Revenue Code

1980

For the calendar year 1980, or tax year beginning _____ 1980 and ending _____ , 19 ___

Please type, print, or attach label. See Specific Instructions	**Name of organization**
	Address (number and street)
	City or town, State, and ZIP code

Employer identification number

If the foundation is in a 60-month termination under section 507(b)(1)(B) check here . ▶ ☐

Fair market value of assets at end of year

If address changed, check here ▶ ☐   Foreign organizations, check here ▶ ☐

The books are in care of ▶ ....
Located at ▶   Telephone no. ▶

If exemption application is pending, check here . . . ▶ ☐

Part I	Analysis of Revenue and Expenses (See instructions for Part I)	(A) Revenue and expenses per books	(B) Computation of net investment income	(C) Computation of adjusted net income	(D) Disbursements for exempt purpose
Revenue	1 Gross contributions, gifts, grants, etc. (see instructions) .				
	2 Contributions from split-interest trusts (see instructions) .				
	3 Gross dues and assessments				
	4 Interest				
	5 Dividends				
	6 Gross rents and royalties				
	7 Net gain or (loss) from sale of assets not on line 11 . .				
	8 Capital gain net income (see instructions) . . .				
	9 Net short-term capital gain (see instructions) . .				
	10 Income modifications (see instructions) . . .				
	11 Gross profit from any business activities: (Gross receipts ▶ $............... minus cost of sales ▶ $...............) (see instructions)				
	12 Other income (attach schedule)				
	13 Total—add lines 1 through 12				
Expenses	14 Compensation of officers, etc. (see instructions)				
	15 Other salaries and wages				
	16 (a) Pension plan contributions (enter number of plans ▶.............)				
	(b) Other employee benefits				
	17 Investment, legal, and other professional services				
	18 Interest				
	19 Taxes (see instructions)				
	20 Depreciation, amortization, and depletion (see instructions)				
	21 Rent				
	22 Other expenses (attach schedule)				
	23 Contributions, gifts, grants (see instructions) .				
	24 Total—add lines 14 through 23				
	25 (a) Excess of revenue over expenses: Line 13 minus line 24 . .				
	(b) Net investment income (if negative enter -0-) . .				
	(c) Adjusted net income (see instructions) (if negative enter -0-)				

Part II	Excise Tax On Investment Income

1 Domestic organizations enter 2% of line 25(b). Foreign organizations enter 4% of line 25(b) . . . . . . ____

2 Credits: (a) Foreign organizations—tax withheld at source . . . .
        (b) Tax paid with application for extension of time to file (Form 2758) . . . . . ____

3 Tax due—line 1 minus line 2. Pay in full with return. Make check or money order payable to Internal Revenue Service (write employer identification number on check or money order) . . . . ▶ ____

4 Overpayment—line 2 minus line 1 . . . . ▶ ____

Foreign organization—Enter book value ▶ $ _____ and fair market value ▶ $ _____ of investment assets held in U.S.

Under penalties of perjury, I declare that I have examined this return, including accompanying schedules and statements, and to the best of my knowledge and belief it is true, correct, and complete. Declaration of preparer (other than taxpayer) is based on all information of which the preparer has any knowledge.

Sign Here

▶ Signature of officer or trustee _____ Date _____

▶ Title _____

▶ Preparer's signature _____

▶ Preparer's address (or employer's name and address) _____

Forms suggest order, rationality, bureaucracy, organization, and in the case of tax forms, power.

159

Social codes deal with relations among men and women and cover such areas as signs of identity and rank (uniforms and insignia), rules for polite behavior and good manners, fashion, and so on. Social codes tell people how to behave, in the broadest sense of the term, in the company of others.

Aesthetic codes, on the other hand, deal with the arts and tell us how to interpret and evaluate the arts. We examine the signs in a given work and search for the codes that are "hidden" behind them but which give them force and meaning. According to Guiraud, the more elite or avant-garde arts have less conventional signs, which makes it difficult for people to interpret and understand these works. On the other hand, popular arts work with very conventional signs and are thus easy to understand... but often not particularly interesting. From this point of view, formulas are conventional coding systems that employ conventional signs (such as stereotyped figures, typical situations, etc.).

Finally, we come to logical codes. These involve our attempts to make sense of the world and include scientific knowledge, nonlinguistic communication systems (braille, Morse code, sign language, sephamore systems, nonverbal communication), highway codes, symbolic languages (as in chemistry, symbolic logic), zodiac signs, and so on. In scientific codes there is often an attempt to be as specific as possible and to eliminate ambiguities and confusion created by language.

The various kinds of codes are, it must be emphasized, human inventions and products of culture. Codes are necessary because the relationship between the signifier and signified is arbitrary or conventional. Just as culture is dynamic and changes, so codes change. Scientific codes tend to be relatively static but aesthetic and social codes are continually undergoing change. Our ideas of what is "proper" as far as the relationship that should exist between men and women is a good example of this. Historical developments like the women's liberation movement and technological advances like the pill have radically altered relations between the sexes.

One factor that seems to be particularly important as far as codes are concerned is class level. Basil Bernstein, a distinguished British scholar, has investigated the relation that exists between socioeconomic class and language use in Britain and has come up with some interesting conclusions. He suggests there is a difference between the language codes of middle-class people, which he describes as "elaborated" and the language codes of working-class people, which he describes as "restricted." The difference between these two codes is shown in the following chart:

Elaborated Codes	*Restricted Codes*
Middle Classes	Working Classes
Grammatically Complex	Grammatically Simple

Varied Vocabulary	Uniform Vocabulary
Complex Sentence Structure	Short, Repetitious Sentences
Careful Use of Adjectives and Adverbs	Little Use of Adjectives and Adverbs
Varied Use of Conjunctions	Repetitious Use of Conjunctions
Not Predictable	Predictable
High Level of Conceptualization and Generalization	Low Level of Conceptualization and Generalization
Logical	Emotional
Use of Qualifications	Little Use of Qualifications
Users Aware of the Code	Users Unaware of the Code

Obviously, people using the different codes perceive the world differently and relate to one another in different ways.

These codes function, then, as gatekeepers and play an important part in our lives since they tend to determine what we know of the world and how we operate in it. As Claus Mueller says in *The Politics of Communication*:

> Almost from birth, the individual acquires the language code specific to his group which in turn provides the matrix for all that he can explore in speech and thought. If the available lexical and syntactic resources are underdeveloped and if arrested communication persists, an individual or group will not be able to select freely among existing perceptual and cognitive alternatives. Their ability to generalize and to use an abstract mode of understanding will be limited. In short, they will be unable to exceed cognitively those social relationships from which the code emanates. (1973:58)

Thus people tend to become "locked into" the world their language codes enable them to perceive and deal with, and people with a restricted language code tend to move in a narrow and rather constricted world. The restricted code, I might add, does have certain positive attributes but it is terribly limiting and tends to lead to fatalism and present-mindedness.

From the semiological point of view, baseball is not just a simple game but, rather, a complicated and semiologically interesting activity. And I'm speaking about more than the "signs" that coaches flash runners or catchers give pitchers.

Baseball: Threes, Fours, and Exclusions

Baseball, the so-called "national pastime" of Americans, has (relatively speaking) declined in popularity in recent years, but it is still a game of considerable importance in American society. It is a significant socializing agent here for young boys, who around the age of eight or nine tend to develop what can only be called a mad "passion" for the game. There are, it seems, an almost limitless number of books on great games, great players, great plays, and great teams; for the young devotee, there is a whole history of the game to be learned and an ever-growing mountain of statistics to be learned. Furthermore, at any given moment, the statistics all change. Baseball's dynamism is, for many, more statistical than anything else.

Structurally speaking, baseball is organized around the number three, though there are several instances in which the number four is important. There are three strikes to an out, three outs to an inning, three bases, three basemen, three outfielders and three "units"—the battery, the infield, and the outfield. The number four is important in that four balls mean a batter walks, a homerun means he can "take" three bases and go home, and the shortstop can be seen as the fourth man in the infield, the only one not assigned to a base. Batting averages are also computed on the basis of thousands—that is, to the fourth digit—though the averages are given in terms of three figures.

Multiples of three are also significant, for there are nine players on a team and the standard game goes nine innings, adding up to 54 outs. With rare exceptions, the game is also based upon exclusions. There is only one situation in which some kind of a limiting exclusion is not operating—the case of foul balls. In all other cases, a given action is either one thing or something else. For example, pitched balls are strikes or balls. Batted balls (except for fouls, mentioned earlier) are hits or outs, and even foul balls are often caught for outs. A ball is hit either fair or foul to either the infield or the outfield. Runs are either earned or unearned, and games are won or lost—never tied.

We can see these exclusions more clearly in the following chart:

Exclusions in Baseball

Balls	Strikes
Hits	Outs
Plays	Errors
Infield	Outfield
Foul	Fair
Earned run	Unearned run
Won	Lost
Hold to base	Steal a base

This chart suggests that baseball is basically binary and relatively simple. It is a game full of constraints and with little room for maneuvering, as compared to a game like football, which has many more options. In football, for example, a given play can involve a run, a pass, a kick, or a combination of these actions. Football also, interestingly enough, has a three-four structure similar to that of baseball. A team has three plays to make 10 yards, realistically speaking; though the team is allotted four plays or downs, it is only in unusual situations that the players will try to gain yardage for a first down on a fourth down. Once a football team does gain its 10 yards, it begins again, so there is continual action and stress, especially since time is a factor in the game. In football there are a number of different points to be scored: one, three, or six, depending upon the situation.

In baseball the field is always occupied by the defense—which outnumbers the offense by a ratio of nine-to-one, until a player gets on base. Then the ratio changes and the game becomes much more interesting, since the possibility of a runner stealing a base or of a hitter hitting into a double play arises. There are other complexities in baseball: Pitchers have a variety of pitches to use (curves, sliders, knuckleballs, fastballs, spitters, etc.), and batters can get doubles and triples; but *for the most part baseball is locked into a set of exclusions which lead to its being simple and not particularly interesting as a game.*

One must distinguish between the experience of going to a game and the structure of a game, of course. The brilliance of the green grass (or artificial grass) on the playing fields, the sun, the uniforms, the spectacle—all yield a certain amount of pleasure. Even the leisurely nature of the game pleases many people, who see it as a relaxing diversion and a great accompaniment to beer drinking. And there are times in some baseball games when a great deal of tension is generated—when the game is close, when there are men on base (changing the ratios between the offense and the defense), and when there is something at stake—such as the pennant.

Unfortunately for baseball, however, it is locked into its pattern of exclusions and unfortunate ratios, so that most of the time games are not particularly exciting. In addition, so many games are played that no one game (except at the end of the season in certain cases) means very much, so that winning or losing games is not *that* important. Perhaps we must take the game for what it is—a 19th-century kind of pastoral in which the artistry of the players delights us, but which is structurally unsatisfactory, or—to use the jargon of the game—has "two strikes" against it.

Twenty-two

Characteristics of Codes

In the previous chapter I defined codes, dealt with different levels at which codes exist, and discussed Guiraud's work on social, aesthetic, and logical codes. I also mentioned and considered (briefly) the work of Basil Bernstein on elaborated and restricted codes and argued, in general, that codes are of considerable importance in understanding people and society. A simple exercise shows the importance of codes. Examine the following collections of letters E F D P E F and C D B N C D. They are nonsensical and meaningless until we supply the code that enables them to be understood as the figure below shows:

$$+ 1 \quad \text{E F D P E F}$$
$$\text{D E C O D E}$$
$$- 1 \quad \text{C D B N C D}$$

When we know the code we can unlock the meaning.

In the following material I will consider some characteristics of codes that help explain why codes tend to be so invisible.

1. *Codes Are Characterized by Coherence.* Implicit in the very definition of a code is the notion of coherence, the notion that for a code to be a code

the things it codifies have to be related in some systematic way. We are very close here to the "coherence theory of truth," except that the relations are arbitrary for a given sphere and nothing is necessarily related to anything else, except within the sphere covered by the code. Relations are necessary only because the code defines them that way. The coherence theory of truth of the Absolute Idealists stated that there were degrees of truth, and some truths were more true than others in that they explained more about reality than weak truths did.

If everything is related to everything else as the quotation from *The Study in Scarlet* suggests then knowing anything enables you, ultimately, to know everything. You can work it out for yourself—if, that is, you know *how* everything is related to everything else.

2. *Cultures Are Kinds of Codes.*   Every culture is, in part, or can be thought of as, a collection of codes of conduct which is transmitted from one generation to another. I am using culture here anthropologically—not as some people use the word when they are dealing with aesthetic considerations. Everyone has a culture, then—though not everyone necessarily appreciates ballet, chamber music, poetry, literature, and other art forms which require sophisticated and educated sensibilities. I will consider the terms *culture, codes,* and *culture-codes* to be synonymous for our purposes henceforth.

Cultures provide us with "ways of behaving" in various situations and ways of looking at the world and society and man; these ways all lock together to form a coherent system for each culture (or subculture). We know from the work of Basil Bernstein that children pick up, almost by osmosis it seems, attitudes toward time and themselves and the world by means of the codes hidden in the language of their parents and peers. This leads to the next consideration—codes are covert.

3. *Codes Are Covert.*   People are not aware that their actions (and thoughts) are "governed" or "shaped" by their culture. All of this is unconscious and unrecognized by them. A culture is a code and is, therefore, coherent; it also is "secret"—at least to the people involved. When people become aware of cultural codes they can modify them and arrange them to suit their purposes. In such cases, culture as a code loses its power to shape behavior the way it did before it was discovered.

Pierre Bourdieu uses the notion "cultural unconscious" and explains its relation to individuals as follows:

> It may seem surprising to ascribe to the cultural unconscious the attitudes, aptitudes, knowledge, themes and problems, in short the whole system of categories of perception and thought acquired by the systematic apprenticeship which the school organizes or makes it possible to organize. This is because the creator maintains with his acquired culture, as with his early

culture, a relationship which might be defined according to Nicolai Hartmann as both "carrying" and "being carried" and he is not aware that the culture he possesses possesses him. (1971:161–188)

The relationship between the individual and his culture is a complex one, for he both shapes his culture and is shaped by it. The important point for us to consider, however, is that the individual is frequently "unaware" of the extent to which his culture "possesses him."

4. *Codes Are Concrete.*   For a culture to maintain itself (and I will say something about the problem of change later), it must relate to concrete and specific matters. What do you do when a baby cries? Every culture has an answer for this which is related to the specific situation in which the crying occurs. In one cultural tradition you give him a teaspoon of olive oil; in another you feed him; in another (if it is not four hours since he was last fed) you let him cry, until he passes out from exhaustion.

For a code to work it must be specific; the power of culture codes is directly related to their capacity to help or guide people in different situations, and to give detailed and rigorous rules for any given situation. If a code is not concrete people will start improvising, and when they do, the culture as a coherent system is in danger of falling apart. This, in turn, suggests the next attribute of cultural codes—they must be clear.

5. *Codes Must Have Clarity.*   Not only must codes deal with specific matters in specific ways; people must, to the extent it is possible, understand what they are to do. This need for clarity is connected with the need for concreteness. People must know how they are to deal with particular situations they face at various times. A cookbook would be a good example of the need for concreteness and clarity. It is most specific about the contents of a given recipe and about how the contents are to be combined and cooked. It is also a kind of code, in that certain dishes are combined with others and these combinations—though arbitrary—are seen as correct, somehow.

The English eat great quantities of fish and brussels sprouts, but one does not eat "fish and sprouts" or "fish and carrots" or even "fish and baked potatoes." A national cuisine is a code, also. (Barthes sees cuisine as a "signifying system" with rules of association, exclusion, and so on.) People absorb (literally as well as figuratively) this code and seldom question it. Some people, as the result of travel or marriage to people from different cultures, move beyond their cultural food codes, but most do not.

Thus, this unacknowledged code that we know of as culture must be invisible and yet, at the same time, give clear and unambiguous answers to people with specific problems. This tension within a culture is further complicated by change versus continuity.

6. *Codes Must Have Continuity.*   It is only logical that cultures must have continuity and lasting power, otherwise the very idea of culture and cultural codes is compromised. On the other hand, cultures are subjected to pressures (brought on by social changes, historical accidents, and so on) so they must change, also—but they cannot change too fast lest they lose their identity or coherence. When we use the word "tradition" we are really talking about the continuity of a culture, its capacity to affect people's expectations and ideas about what is correct and valuable.

Cultures face the dilemma, then, of mediating between the internal need for continuity and maintenance and the external pressure to change and accommodate to new situations, which may be a condition for survival. Sometimes this dilemma is solved through the creation of subcultures, which siphon off discontented elements into little entities at variance in certain respects to the main culture but which do not necessarily aim at overthrowing it. Other times, however, countercultures arise which are antagonistic to the central culture and which engage it in a fight for survival—a fight which sometimes is successful, but which frequently leads to minor modifications in the main culture, enabling the latter to weather the storm.

Codes must have continuity but they must also face the need of being changed and probably can be best characterized as being in a state of dynamic equilibrium.

7. *Codes Are Comprehensive.*   Culture strives toward totality; it must cover as much of a given person's world of experience (or a society's) as it can. It is this comprehensiveness which helps account for its invisibility. Because culture is everywhere we take no notice of it; it is a case of fish not being aware of water: it is their total environment, and so becomes invisible—they cannot get away from it and take it into account.

This comprehensiveness is implicit in the definition of a code. A code that did not tell how to understand every figure or word group in a coded message would not be very useful, though a good cryptologist could no doubt deduce or derive the whole code from knowing part of it. Cultural codes are a different matter, however. Within their sphere (nations, regions, classes, and so on) they must be comprehensive in order to function without being noticed.

Let us return to our example of food systems or codes. Not only do we pick up from the code ideas about what foods are good to eat and what foods go with other foods, we also gain notions about the order in which foods should be served, how a "complete" meal should be started and ended. In America, for example, we don't serve boiled potatoes with steak, and we broil steaks rather than boil them. We serve soup before steak and potatoes, not after; and we generally have something sweet for "dessert," not something sour, and not soup. We usually have, codified in cookbooks, a comprehensive plan for eating during a given day which nobody thinks twice about. My use of cookbooks as an example suggests another aspect of codes—they are communicated.

8. *Codes Are Communicated.*   All of the points I have been making about codes are implicit in the definition of codes, and so is the notion of communication as being central to codes. If, for example, codes are "reflected" in signs and symbols (which would mean there are symbol systems), then they function as useful clues to the cryptologist who is trying to "break" cultural codes—especially if codes are also coherent and comprehensive.

Much mass-communication work is involved in searching for clues—what George Gerbner calls "cultural indicators"—to codes and to reconstituting the codes from bits and pieces which become unmasked and are revealed as existing and as affecting people. Content analysis, for example, is a very explicit attempt to find codes by searching for hidden patterns that exist in the material being studied. Students of literature are interested in codes from another perspective—that of the relationship between artistic technique and the culture, though at times they make content analyses and use other tools of mass-communciation research.

All forms of communication (language, gesture, music, painting, and whatever kind you can think of) have a relation to the culture in which they are found; they mediate between the code and the individual, and that code is something that can be searched for and, it is hoped, discovered—at least in part. These communications involve such matters as assumptions people have, their values, logic, and superstitions, their myths and legends, their "high culture" and their "popular culture." It may very well be that different disciplines, like the blind men and the elephant, spend their time with discipline-specific aspects of a code or codes, and the movement for interdisciplinary studies represents an attempt, not fully realized or understood, to crack as much of the code as possible.

This is probably an impossible goal, since codes and cultures are in process and continually changing, but it seems likely that much more can be done with codes than has been done. It may even be that the semioticians have come closer (or, at least, have the opportunity to do so) than anyone else to cracking the various codes, but in order to understand the semiologists you have to crack *their* codes, which is often no simple matter.

All of us, whether we are aware of it or not, spend a great deal of time decoding signs. If you don't know the correct code you are likely to misinterpret the sign. We are all obliged, then, to search for the codes that will help us interpret in the correct manner the signs we consider important.

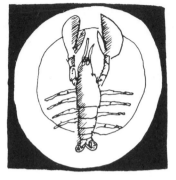

Recently a neighbor had my wife and me over for dinner. She served a delicious and beautiful rack of lamb (cooked to perfection with the lamb pink, the fat brown). This meal, like all meals, was more than food: it was, in addition, a sign of affection, of esteem. Foods vary in terms of their status—steak has higher status than hamburger, for instance, so when we are invited out for dinner, we can gain a sense of what our hosts think of us when we find out what we are being served. Foods are signs (and though I don't explore the matter here, dining out in fancy restaurants is theatre).

FOODS AS SIGNS

Recently a book was published in London listing cheap places to eat; the criterion was, to put it bluntly, "how much food for how little expense." Its title, *Fuel Food*, captures an attitude toward food that many people have. Food is fuel for the body-machine and food's basic function is to keep us going, so we can work hard, play hard, and do whatever else we care to do.

From this point of view, eating is not a source of sensual pleasure and delight but is, instead, functional and obligatory. This fuelish notion is, I would suggest, a residue of ascetic Protestantism, which has shaped our minds to a great extent, and now, we discover, our bodies. Our attitudes in America have been influenced by our Puritan heritage, which has not only affected our sexuality but also our food preferences.

In a remarkable essay called "Gastrosophy" (the philosophy of food), the celebrated Mexican poet and writer Octavio Paz investigated American food and came to some fascinating conclusions. (*Daedalus*, Fall 1972) The adjectives he uses to describe our food tell a story. Our cuisine, he says, is "simple," "spiceless," "honest," and based on "exclusions," just like our culture. Our food "ignores ambiguity and ambivalence," and our beverages (such as gin and whiskey) accentuate "withdrawal" and "unsociability."

Paz compares American food with Mexican and French food, both of which he says involve blendings, transubstantiations, and mysteries. Compared to these cuisines, American food—with its emphasis on purity and a passion for milk and ice cream (pregenital innocence)—is rather tasteless and bland. We might say that *in America dining has been replaced by eating.* Instead of meals being socializing experiences and happy occasions, we tend to look upon meals as interruptions. There are millions of families who hardly ever eat a meal together; people grab what they can in passing and the members of the family don't see one another around the dining-room table, or anyplace else, for that matter.

The whole fast-food industry, as symbolized by McDonald's, represents, if you think about it, an attitude toward food; the mechanization and technologizing of food has a grimness and alienating quality about it that is profoundly disturbing to many people. On the other hand, there is an increasing interest in gourmet cooking, but this is limited, it seems, to a small, number of educated, "sophisticated" elements in the population. And even the lovers of gourmet food treat good dining as something exceptional.

Attitudes toward food are essentially cultural. English food is, as a rule, undistinguished at best; eating seems to be unimportant to the English, while 12 miles across the channel, the French seem to have made eating one of the focal points of their lives. Statistics show that the French spend more time eating—an average of 106 minutes a day—than anyone else. They also spend a lot of time sleeping (time spent sleeping correlates with time spent eating), leading some to describe the French as having an "eat–sleep" culture

Although we seldom think about it, every person carries around in his or her head attitudes and beliefs about food that determine how and what he or she eats. We all have certain codes and principles of organization that we use when we plan a meal: that is what a cuisine is. We pick up, *though we are unaware of it,* preferences and rules of combination which affect what we eat. For example, though the English eat great quantities of brussel sprouts and carrots and fried fish, you do not see "Fish and Sprouts" shops or "Fish and Carrots" shops because we all know that fish goes with chips and nothing else.

Different foods and different kinds of foods have different statuses. When people are invited out to dinner it is not unusual for them to speculate about what will be served. The reason we do so is to determine how highly our company is valued, how much esteem we are to be granted. Generally speaking, I would suggest that the following chart distinguishes between high-and low-status foods in America.

According to this scheme roast beef and steak are "signs" that have very high ratings, while stews and hamburger are dishes that have relatively low status; and duck or pheasant, being uncommon, have more status than chicken. When gourmet cooking is involved, the ranking

Status of Foods in America

High-Status Foods	Low-Status Foods
whole items that can be carved	pieces of food already cut up or ground
red meat (steak, roast beef)	white meat (chicken, fish)
roasted, broiled	fried, boiled
uncommon (pheasant)	common (chicken)
served natural	served covered with gravy or sauce
large	small
homemade	bottled or canned
identity kept	identity disguised (turned into something else)
individual preferences count (rare)	mass production
bloody	no blood

system doesn't work perfectly because we have now introduced a foreign element into our considerations. Veal, which is highly regarded in Europe is not esteemed in this country. If you serve your guests a dish using veal they will find it difficult to estimate what you think of them. Veal confounds because it is an unclear sign.

Deciding the status of meals is frequently taken care of for us in restaurants; there, the price of the items gives them their status and what you order gives you your status in the waiter's mind. In fancy restaurants where waiters are often tyrants and snobs, a great deal of pressure is exerted upon us to order expensive dishes and prove that we "belong." Unfortunately, as many of us keep finding out, in gourmet restaurants in America we tend to consume "style" or "signs" rather than superb food.

Although food is one of those subjects most people tend to take for granted, it is a subject of immense importance. Anthropologists have been engaged in food research for many years and are now involved with "deciphering" meals—analyzing them in terms of their principles of organization rather than in terms of what is being served.

If you think food is important, you must look at the supermarket in an entirely different way. It is not so much a story but, rather, a mass medium of staggering cultural significance. It "broadcasts" food in the same manner that McDonald's, Burger King, and so on broadcast hamburgers. The fact that both the supermarkets and fast-food joints are broadcasting so much hamburger has considerable importance. I call this phenomenon the hamburgeoisement of the masses—fooling people into believing they have eaten meat and are middle class. Here we have the digestive system and the socioeconomic system meeting in the hamburger system.

Twenty-three

Meaning

Have you ever wondered why it is that often when you think of a word the opposite of the word pops into your head? There is a reason for this. It is because meaning is relational. *Nothing means anything in itself* and everything means something because of some kind of a relationship in which it is embedded. This relationship can be obvious or it can be implied, but one way or another it must be there. (I am speaking here of concepts.)

Thus "rich" only has meaning if there is "poor" and "large" only has meaning if there is "small." An object, for example, is only large relative to some other object. A man is "large" compared to an ant but "small" compared to a mountain. As Saussure wrote, "concepts are purely differential and defined not by their positive content but negatively by their relations with the other terms of the system." (1966:117) Jonathan Culler put this another way when he wrote in *Structuralist Poetics:*

> Structuralists have generally followed Jakobson and taken the binary opposi-
> tion as a fundamental operation of the human mind basic to the production of
> meaning: "this elementary logic which is the smallest common denominator of
> all thought." (1975:15)

In the case of words this is fairly obvious. Binary or polar oppositions do not occur simply by chance; they are, if Jakobson is correct, basic to the operation of the human mind.

We are all, then, somewhat like computers—computers also work on the principle of binary oppositions. Our concern as sign interpreters is to find the relationships that exist between signs and something else: concepts, attitudes, feelings, mental states, and so on. Oppositions are also to be found in narratives where we finds, for example, "good guys" and "bad guys," rich men and poor men, people living "upstairs" and "downstairs." These oppositions may not always be obvious or evident but they are always there. This is because, in part, stories need to be exciting and excitement is based in large measure on conflict and conflict implies oppositions of one kind or another. When we deal with texts we must elicit the various paired oppositions that give these texts meaning.

For example, the following oppositions help us understand what is going on in "Upstairs, Downstairs," the British television series that was so popular in America in recent years:

Upstairs	*Downstairs*
Wealthy	Poor
Masters (command)	Servants (obey)
Educated	Uneducated (but often shrewd)
Leisure	Hard work
Openness	Closure
Space	Crowdedness
Champagne	Beer
Marriage	Bachelorhood
Infidelity	Fidelity

These oppositions inform the series and give it meaning. Even if the series had been called "The Bellamys" it would still have been based on the upstairs–downstairs opposition and everything that followed from that opposition.

This oppositional structure which we search for in narratives is called the "paradigmatic" structure and gives us what Lévi-Strauss calls the *latent* (or hidden) meaning of texts. Just as signs have latent meanings, as I suggested in my discussion of cocktail signs for bars, so texts have latent meanings. When we elicit these meanings we discover what the narrative is "really" about.

I might point out that this concern with oppositions is nothing new. In *Opposition*, C. K. Ogden deals with a variety of aspects of the phenomenon and mentions that Aristotle was "obsessed" with the problem:

> The subject of Opposition has a long and respectable history, for Aristotle himself was obsessed by the problem of opposition which appears in different

forms in all his works, though the special treatise which he devoted to it has not survived.

In the *Metaphysics* he deals with the oppositions of Unity and Multiplicity, Being and Not-being. All philosophers, he says, recognize that the principles are contraries; some refer to the Odd and the Even, others to Hot and Cold, others to the Finite and the Infinite, others again to Love and Discord:—but all these can be reduced to Unity *versus* Multiplicity. Later he opposes the Anterior and the Posterior, Genus and Species, the Whole and the Part, and is troubled about the Small and the Great, the Straight and the Curved, etc. He regards everything as proceeding from contraries.... (1976:21)

Those interested in pursuing this would do well to read *Opposition,* which also deals with other aspects of the phenomenon.

There is, of course, the danger of reductionism involved with binarism; that seems quite obvious and Culler discusses the problem. One final caution about the construction of the polar oppositions in texts: the terms should be true oppositions and not just negations (rich, non-rich).

In the following chart I list some of our more interesting oppositions (and where useful, names associated with them).

Important Oppositions

The One	The Many (Plato)
Masculine	Feminine
Light	Dark
Good	Evil
Potentiality	Actuality
Raw	Cooked (Lévi-Strauss)
I	Thou (Buber)
Subject	Object
Sacred	Profane (Eliade)
Body	Mind
Past	Future
Conscious	Unconscious (Freud)
Qualitative	Quantitative
Active	Passive
Elite	Common
Bourgeois	Proletarian (Marx)
Nature	History
Idealism	Materialism
Thesis	Antithesis (Hegel)
Ascetic	Hedonistic
Acid	Alkali
Digital	Analog
Gesellschaft	Gemeinschaft (Tönnies)

Yin	Yang
Classical	Romantic
Totalitarian	Anarchistic
Existence	Essence (Kierkegaard)
Dionysian	Apollonian
Physical	Mental
Superficial	Profound
Positive	Negative
Hierarchy	Equality
Work	Play
Pleasure	Pain
Love	Hate
Electronic	Mechanical
Spiritual	Material
Flexible	Rigid
Western	Eastern
Beginning	End
Action	Reaction
Heaven	Hell

It is simply remarkable how great a role these oppositions (and a few dozen others that might be listed) have played in history and in culture. This is to be expected since, as Saussure put it, "in language there are only differences." Meaning arises from relationships and the most important relationship is that of opposition. We may not be aware of the relations in any given situation, and there may be a mediating concept in some situations (such as the ego which mediates between the demands of the id and the superego) but where there is meaning there is opposition.

In this essay The Paper Chase *is analyzed in terms of the bipolar oppositions found in it which, in theory, generate the meaning people find in the series. The focus here is not on plot, or what happens, but on meaning.*

THE PAPER CHASE VS. THE RATINGS GAME*

With few exceptions, the new television series "The Paper Chase" has been favorably received by the television critics. Some have even suggested it might be the best new series this year—a year which, remember, has brought us W.E.B., "Vegas," "WKRP" (are they trying to tell us something here?), "The Mary Tyler Moore Show," "Mork and Mindy," and so on. Some of these shows died very quickly, others are lingering, and a few seem to be "hits." Despite its critical success, "The Paper Chase" does not seem to have much of a future. Placed in the same time slot as "Laverne and Shirley" and "Happy Days," one would almost have to say that "The Paper Chase" is being offered as a sacrificial victim to the voracious god, Media Ratings.

(In San Francisco, for example, during the week of October 7–13, "The Paper Chase" had a 7 rating and 10 share, "Happy Days" had a 10 rating and 30 share, and "Laverne and Shirley" had a 28 rating and a 41 share. The rating measures the percentage of the Bay Area market and the share measures the percentage of those watching television at the time. It is generally held that a program has to get a 30 share to stay alive, so "The Paper Chase" may not last too much longer. It was scheduled opposite "Happy Days" and "Laverne and Shirley," two "bubblegum shows," to provide an alternative for those people interested in better quality programming. Not too many people are availing themselves of this opportunity.)

* Published by permission of Transaction, Inc. from SOCIETY, Vol. 16 #2. Copyright ©
1979 by Transaction, Inc.

The program deals with the difficulties a group of law-school students face in their "chase" to get their degree—the piece of paper that means so much to them. The ambience is Ivy League. The students are, for the most part, attractive, intelligent, and hard working. But before they can get through their first year of law school they must survive an ordeal—they must take a course in contract law with Professor Charles W. Kingsfield, Jr., an individual who has terrorized students for decades.

His classroom is a sacred space, a privileged area where Kingsfield instructs his novitiates in the intricacies of contract law. Although different members of the cast are featured each week in some adventure relating to their personal lives, it is around Kingsfield that the series revolves. He is a larger-than-life presence who dominates the thoughts—and, at times, dreams—of his students.

Although the portrayal of law school in "The Paper Chase" is not very realistic, the program does show the kind of pressure that builds up in universities where there is great competition for good grades and there are frequently very destructive relationships. In the program it is Kingsfield who puts incredible pressure on the students and forces them to memorize enormous amounts of material and have it available for immediate recall. In most law schools it is the students themselves who generate most of the pressure, as they fight for grades, memberships on the law reviews, and that kind of thing. But whatever the locus of the pressure might be, there is often a great deal of tension in the halls of academe.

If young people are willing to undergo such ordeals, which threaten their physical health and mental well-being, the rewards must be enormous. That is the logical conclusion we draw from watching the program. That paper must really be worth something. And that seems to be the case. The lawyers we see in the program generally are very wealthy, live in huge homes, and having survived Kingsfield and made their way out of his labyrinth of contract law, seem to find the outside world a bowl of cherries.

Kingsfield is a tutelary figure who initiates young people into the "mysteries" of law. Like all demigods he is stern and uncompromising, but all of this, we know, is for the students' own good. He will produce lawyers whose minds have been honed as sharp as razors. All the memorizing and terrorizing serve, then, an ulterior purpose—to create heroic personalities who having survived their ordeal are ready to serve mankind. The lawyer becomes a mythic hero, armed with an encyclopedia of facts and figures, who has been tested and not found wanting.

Surveys show that large numbers of Americans fear lawyers and have very little idea, actually, of what they do. What we know of them stems to a great degree from the media and from the world of popular culture. Certain lawyers, usually criminal lawyers, are featured when there is a big trial, and figures on the amount of money these men make are often carried in the press. Thus we tend to have a highly distorted image of what lawyers are like, and tend to be afraid to use them since we fear they will cost more than we can afford—or they are worth.

Now we can watch "The Paper Chase" and see the way law-school students suffer. When they get out of law school they will want recompense for their ordeals and we fear it will be at our expense. (Is it not a coincidence that both doctors and lawyers—our two great mythic heroes from the professional world—are both put through ordeals and servitude before they are unleashed on society, full of anger and resentment and knowing a great deal about the paper-chase game.) Is it any wonder that we are full of fear and anxiety when dealing with these people who have a head full of arcane knowledge and whose minds have been formed in remarkable ways by mentors such as Kingsfield?

I have suggested, to this point, that "The Paper Chase" has a mythical and mystifying dimension to it. It deals with the quest theme, which is a traditional one in American culture, and it suggests that achievement is connected to effort (which sometimes reaches the level of the ordeal) and renunciation of momentary pleasures in favor of deferred but more rewarding pleasures. Knowledge is power. If you'd ever wondered whether that was true, "The Paper Chase" will put your mind to rest on that issue. And once by Kingsfield, the Minotaur of contract law, law students will have proven themselves worthy of using this power.

The meaning of the program stems from oppositions which are embedded in it and which are connected to our value system. Kingsfield represents age and wisdom. He is a sage who teaches, in his own inimitable manner, and his authority is based on his knowledge and his achievements—volumes of books on his speciality. He stands for tradition, for logic and reason—though, curiously, he is, himself, quite unreasonable and terribly demanding. He is an elite figure and a distant one, a character who represents the East coast in the public mind. That would certainly explain his "driven" nature. He might have stepped out of the Puritan holy commonwealth and could well be a distant relation to a character like Cotton Mather. He is a representation of "the head" and shows the danger of intellect untempered by mercy, though we all know that underneath that gruff exterior there is great love.

And on the other side of the equation what do we find? Hart! Well named, too. Hart comes from the Midwest, which means he is a natural person, one of what we used to call "nature's noblemen." He is also poor, and is working his way through law school as a waiter, which means he is a classic Horatio Alger figure who shows that success is available to anyone who has willpower, determination, and courage. Hart is one of a number of students who, collectively, balance Kingsfield. They represent youth and potentiality, they are learning, they are being initiated, they are close to one another and have feelings and emotions, they live in a state of terror, and they are figures of the moment. All of these attributes found in the students have meaning because of Kingsfield and all that he stands for.

Let me show these relationships in the following chart:

Kingsfield	Students
Head	Hart (Heart)
Age	Youth
Wisdom	Innocence
Authority	Equality
Achievement	Potentiality
Initiator	Initiated
Logic, Reason	Emotions, Feelings
Distance	Closeness
Terrorist	Terrorized
The East Coast	The Real America
Tradition	The Moment

It is Kingsfield's mission, as he sees it, to preserve the great tradition of the East, of Puritan conscience and morality in a society in which these virtues are under attack by the forces of personal greed and a debased pragmatic acceptance of whatever it is that sells. Kingsfield is an anachronism and John Houseman's portrayal is a marvelous rendering of a figure battling heroically in what seems to be a lost cause.

Is this stern Puritanical figure what we need to hold the line against the demons of immorality and unscrupulousness, or is Kingsfield a relic of a past full of demonic and perverted figures who are best forgotten? The question, as the lawyers would put it, is probably moot, since unless the program is changed to a different time slot or some kind of a miracle happens, "The Paper Chase" will probably not last much longer. Kingsfield may terrorize his students and fascinate a number of television viewers, but the gallant old aristocrat seems doomed to fall victim to the likes of "Laverne and Shirley." Television vice-presidents, it so happens, also live in terror and play the game of the ratings chase. (That's what the short-lived "W.E.B." was about.)

Not only does "The Paper Chase" reveal a great deal about American culture, its fate will also tell a lot about the kind of society in which we live. There's not much room, anymore, for aristocrats or royalists (the name Kingsfield is significant in this respect) except in some of our more elite universities, and even there they seem to have become irrelevant. In many respects this is a great loss.

References

Allen, Woody. "Spring Bulletin." *The New Yorker*, April 29, 1967.

Barthes, Roland. 1972. *Mythologies*. New York: Hill and Wang.

_____. 1982. *Empire of Signs*. New York: Hill and Wang.

Becker, Stephen. 1959. *Comic Art in America*. New York: Simon and Schuster.

Berger, John. 1972. *Ways of Seeing*. London: British Broadcasting Corporation and Penguin Books.

Boggs, Joseph. 1978. *The Art of Watching Films*. Menlo Park, Ca.: Benjamin Cummings.

Bourdieu, Pierre "Intellectual Field and Creative Project." In Michael F.D. Young, ed., *Knowledge and Control*. London: Collier-MacMillan, 1971.

Carter, David E. 1975. *Designing Corporate Symbols*. Ashland, Ky.: Century Communications.

Cawelti, John. 1971. *The Six-Gun Mystique*. Bowling Green, Ohio: Popular Press.

Coward, Rosalind, and Ellis, John. 1977. *Language and Materialism*. London: Routledge and Kegan Paul.

Culler, Jonathan. 1975. *Structuralist Poetics*. Ithaca, N.Y.: Cornell University Press.

Defoe, Daniel. 1946 *Robinson Crusoe*. New York: Grosset & Dunlap.

de Saussure, Ferdinand. 1966. *A Course in General Linguistics*. New York: McGraw Hill.

Dichter, Ernest. 1964. *The Handbook of Consumer Motivations.* New York: McGraw-Hill.

Dostoyevsky, Fyodor. 1945. *Crime and Punishment,* Trans., Constance Garnett. New York: Illustrated Modern Library.

Doyle, A. Conan. 1975. *The Adventures of Sherlock Holmes.* New York: A & W Visual Library.

————. 1969. "A Study in Scarlet." In *The Annotated Sherlock Holmes*, vol. 1, William S. Baring-Gould, ed. New York: Clarkson N. Porter.

Eco, Umberto. 1976. *A Theory of Semiotics.* Bloomington: Indiana University Press.

Eliade, Mircea. 1961. *The Sacred and the Profane.* New York: Harper and Row.

————. 1967. *Myths, Dreams and Mysteries.* New York: Harper and Row.

Freud, Sigmund. 1953. *A General Introduction to Psychoanalysis.* Garden City, N.Y.: Permabooks.

————. 1963. *Character and Culture.* New York: Collier Books.

————. 1963. *Jokes and Their Relation to the Unconscious.* New York: Norton.

————. 1965. *The Interpretation of Dreams.* New York: Avon.

Geertz, Clifford. 1973. *The Interpretation of Cultures.* New York: Basic Books.

Goffman, Erving. 1959. *The Presentation of Self in Everyday Life.* New York: Anchor Books.

Guiraud, Pierre. 1975. *Semiology.* London: Routledge and Kegan Paul.

Hinsie, Leland, and Campbell, R. J. 1970. *Psychiatric Dictionary*, 4th ed. New York: Oxford University Press.

Horn, Maurice. ed. *The World Encyclopedia of Comics.* 1970. New York: Chelsea House Publishers.

Klapp, Orrin E. 1963. *The Collective Search for Identity.* New York: Holt, Rinehart and Winston.

Lippard, Lucy. 1966. *Pop Art.* New York: Praeger.

Martin, Bernice. 1981. *A Sociology of Contemporary Cultural Charge,* New York: St. Martin's Press.

Mehrabian, Albert. 1971. *Silent Messages.* Belmont, Ca.: Wadsworth.

Mueller, Claus. 1973. *The Politics of Communication.* New York: Oxford University Press.

Nathan, Peter E., and Harris, S. L. 1975. *Psychopathology and Society.* New York: McGraw Hill.

Nichols, Bill, ed. 1976. *Movies and Methods.* Berkeley: University of California Press.

Ogden, C. K. 1976. *Opposition.* Bloomington: Indiana University Press.

Peirce, C. S. 1958. *The Collected Papers of C.S. Peirce*, vols. 1–6, Charles Hartshorne and Paul Weiss, eds., 1931–5; vols. 7–8, A.W. Burks, ed., 1958. Cambridge: Harvard University Press.

Rublowsky, John. 1965. *Pop Art.* New York: Basic Books.

Sapirstein, Milton 1955. *Paradoxes of Everyday Life.* Greenwich, Conn.: Premier Books.

Scholes, Robert. 1974. *Structuralism in Literature.* New Haven, Conn.: Yale University Press.

Shakespeare, William. 1966. *Henry the Fourth, Part I.* W. W. Norton & Co. New York.

Sebeok, T. 1977. *A Perfusion of Signs.* Bloomington: Indiana University Press.

Sypher, Wylie. 1956. *Comedy.* Garden City, N. Y.: Doubleday Anchor Books.

Tindall, William York. 1955. *The Literary Symbol.* Bloomington: Indiana University Press.

Wilson, Robert N., ed. 1964. *The Arts in Society.* Englewood Cliffs, N. J.: Prentice-Hall.

Winick, Charles. 1968. *The New People.* New York: Pegasus.

Wolfe, Tom. 1966. *The Kandy-Kolored Tangerine-Flake Streamline Baby.* New York: Pocket Books.

Wollen, Peter. 1972. *Signs and Meaning in the Cinema.* Bloomington: Indiana University Press.

Zettl, Herbert. 1973. *Sight, Sound, Motion.* Belmont, Ca.: Wadsworth.

A Selected Bibliography

Barthes, Roland. *Writing Degree Zero and Elements of Semiology*. Boston: Beacon Press, 1970. In *Elements of Semiology* Barthes offers a technical exposition of some of the most fundamental concepts found in semiological theory. The book is divided into four parts: Language (Langue) and Speech; Signifier and Signified; Syntagm and System; and Denotation and Connotation. Barthes also makes reference to his work on fashion, food, furniture, advertising, and so on, but there is very little applied semiological analysis in this book.

Barthes, Roland. *Mythologies*. New York: Hill and Wang, 1972. This book is one of Barthes's most celebrated studies and offers the typical Barthesian combination of beautiful writing and astonishing insights. The first part of the book is devoted to semiological analyses of such topics as wrestling, detergents, margarine, toys, plastic, the strip-tease, etc. Barthes reveals the significance of these objects and activities, using concepts from semiological theory. He attempts to demythologize mass culture and expose its ideological content, among other things. The second part of the book is devoted to a theoretical analysis, from a semiological and Marxist perspective, of "Myth Today."

Coward, Rosalind and John Ellis. *Language and Materialism: Developments in Semiology and the Theory of the Subject*. London: Routledge and Kegan Paul, 1977. This influential book deals with semiological theory and its relationship to Lacan's rereading of Freud and Marxist theories of ideology. Central to all considerations is language, and, in particular, the sign ... which forms the basis of the reinterpretation offered by Coward and Ellis of the ideas of Freud and Marx.

Culler, Jonathan. *Structuralist Poetics: Structuralism, Linguistics and the Study of Literature*. Ithaca, New York: Cornell University Press, 1975. An outstanding explanation of the basic principles of semiological thought and application of these principles to literature. It also contains a 20-page bibliography of important articles and books on structuralism. Culler has also written a superb book on the ideas of Saussure and other works on semiological subjects.

de Saussure, Ferdinand. *Course in General Linguistics*. New York: McGraw-Hill, 1966. This classic text, reconstructed from lecture notes by students and others, opened the door for the development of semiology. Many of the central concepts in semiology were elaborated by Saussure: the division of the sign into the signifier and the signified, the distinction between synchronic and diachronic analysis, the distinction between language and speech, and so on. In this book Saussure called for the development of a science that would be called semiology and would study the "life of signs within society."

Eco, Umberto. *A Theory of Semiotics*. Bloomington: Indiana University Press, 1976. This book is one of the most important theoretical works in semiotics of recent years and required reading for all serious students of the subject. It is just one of a series of works, theoretical and applied, by the man who, with the death of Barthes, is probably the most important and most influential semiotician alive. In addition to his popular essays in the Italian press, Eco has written what might be called a "semiotic" novel, *The Name of the Rose,* which has won numerous awards and is a best seller in Europe. *A Theory of Semiotics* is a demanding and difficult book which should not be attempted until the reader has read a number of other books and has gained some understanding of the subject.

Elam, Keir. *The Semiotics of Theatre and Drama*. London: Methuen, 1980. Elam offers a discussion of the basic principles of semiotics and then a treatment of the semiological codes which underlie theatrical performances of all kinds. Once we understand Elam's ideas about dramatalogical analysis, we can apply them to traditional drama and theatre, but also to other forms of theatre such as television commercials, appliance demonstrators in department stores, stand-up comedians, and lecturers. The book features a fascinating analysis of the first 79 lines of Shakespeare's *Hamlet.* Elam's analysis draws heavily on the work of Eco and the Prague School.

Fiske, John and John Hartley *Reading Television*. London: Methuen, 1978. One of the basic values of this book lies in its semiological interpretations (or "readings") of a number of specific television programs and its discussion of the "bardic" functions of television. Among the television programs it analyzes are "The News at Ten," "Come Dancing," and "The Generation Game" (all British programs). The book devotes a considerable amount of discussion to communication theory and sociological aspects of the mass media.

Guiraud, Pierre. *Semiology*. London: Routledge and Kegan Paul, 1975. We have here a short (106 pages) primer on semiology that focuses on logical, aesthetic, and social codes which, Guiraud shows, are central to much of our experience.

Thus, in his examination of social codes, he brings interesting perspectives to bear on such matters as insignia, manners, proxemics, protocols, rituals, fashions, and games—all of which can be interpreted and better understood by using semiological principles.

Hawkes, Terence. *Structuralism and Semiotics.* Berkeley: University of California Press, 1977. This text is one of the most useful introductions to semiotics. It has chapters on Saussure, Lévi-Strauss, the Russian Formalists, Roland Barthes, Roman Jakobson, and a number of other important semioticians. A lucid and comprehensive overview which serves as an excellent means of surveying the subject. Recommended as a first book in semiotics because of its clarity and comprehensiveness.

Jameson, Frederick. *The Prison-House of Language: a Critical Account of Structuralism and Russian Formalism.* Princeton, N.J.: Princeton University Press, 1972. A well-argued and lucid examination of Russian Formalism and French structuralism. Jameson has interesting things to say about the work of Roland Barthes and Claude Lévi-Strauss (among others) and about the relationship that exists between structuralism and Marxism. The book also serves as an introduction to the work of many important French and continental thinkers.

Lavers, Annette. *Roland Barthes: Structuralism and After.* Cambridge, Mass.: Harvard University Press, 1982. This is probably the definitive study of Barthes, a beautifully written, authoritative analysis of his work and his relation to other semioticians. It features detailed and critical examinations of Barthes' most important works. Lavers shows how singular and important Barthes' contribution was. The book also contains an appendix on structuralism and related subjects and an up-to-date and comprehensive bibliography on semiotics.

MacCannell, Dean and Juliet Flower MacCannell. *The Time of the Sign: a Semiotic Interpretation of Modern Culture.* Bloomington: Indiana University Press, 1982. The MacCannells have written a provocative book which argues, in essence, that semiotics is needed to rescue the social sciences and liberal arts from stultification and wrong-headedness. They see semiotics as the most useful method of integrating the social sciences and humanities and making them relevant. They call for a semiotic reinterpretation of sociology and anthropology and suggest that the three central intellectual domains in contemporary culture are Freudianism, Marxism, and semiotics. Thus the current epoch is, they suggest, "the time of the sign."

Pettit, Philip. *The Concept of Structuralism: a Critical Analysis.* Berkeley: University of California Press, 1975. A somewhat philosophical analysis of structuralism divided into four chapters: "The Linguistic Model," "The Range of the Model," "A Development of the Model," "The Value of the Model." Pettit describes his book as a "theoretical" essay (and not a historical one) concerned, primarily, with the concept of structuralism and not with the structuralist movement. Of particular interest is his third chapter which is devoted to a criticism of the work of Lévi-Strauss.

Robey, David, ed. *Structuralism: An Introduction.* Oxford, England: Oxford University Press, 1973. The chapters in this book were originally given as the Wolfson College Lectures at Oxford in 1972. Some of the most important figures in semiotic thought are represented here: Jonathan Culler on "The

Linguistic Basis of Structuralism," Edmund Leach on "Structuralism in Social Anthropology," Umberto Eco on "Social Life as a Sign System," Robin Gandy on "'Structure' in Mathematics," and so on. The book is useful not only as an introduction to semiotics but because it suggests the enormous range of semiotics.

Scholes, Robert. *Structuralism in Literature: An Introduction*. New Haven, Conn.: Yale University Press, 1974. As its title suggests, this book is concerned, chiefly, with applying structuralist theory to literature. It deals with important concepts, has material on linguistics, theories of a number of French and continental thinkers (Propp, Lévi-Strauss, the Russian Formalists, Barthes, and others) and is a very useful book for those interested in how semiotic thought can be applied to narrative theory, myth, and to literary texts of all kinds. Scholes provides, among other things, a fascinating structural analysis of Joyce's *Ulysses* and a bibliographical appendix which is really an annotated bibliography on structuralism and literary theory and criticism.

Sebeok, Thomas A., ed. *A Perfusion of Signs*. Bloomington: Indiana University Press, 1977. Sebeok, one of the central figures of the semiotics movement in American academic life, provides here a wide-ranging collection of essays that deal both with semiotic theory and the application of semiotics to various aspects of life: medicine, architecture, music, the circus, culture theory, and so on. This book, and the companion volume that Sebeok edited, *Sight, Sound and Sense* (Indiana University Press, 1978) feature first-class articles by leading semioticians that cover a wide range of topics—from Peirce's theories to nonsense, religion, facial expression, and problems of translation. The books are recommended for those interested in reading authoritative treatments of semiotic theory and its applications by writers, including Umberto Eco, Paul Ekman, Paul Bouissac, Rulon Wells and Thomas Sebeok.

Shukman, Ann. *Literature and Semiotics: a Study of the Writings of Yuri M. Lotman*. Amsterdam: North-Holland Publishing Company, 1977. Yuri Lotman is one of the great figures in contemporary semiotic thought and this study provides the reader with an introduction and analysis of his work and the Moscow–Tartu school of semiotic analysis associated with Lotman. Of particular interest is the work of Lotman and his colleagues on culture in addition to their work on the nature of artistic texts.

Williamson, Judith. *Decoding Advertisements: Ideology and Meaning in Advertising*. London: Marion Boyars, 1978. Williamson offers a combination structuralist and ideological analysis of advertisements, which are, she suggests, "one of the most important cultural factors moulding and reflecting our life today." The book contains reproductions of a number of magazine advertisements and very sophisticated analyses or "readings" of these ads. The book will be of particular interest to those interested in applying semiotics to the mass media and popular culture.

Wollen, Peter. *Signs and Meaning in the Cinema*. Bloomington: Indiana University Press, 1972. Wollen's book is one of the earliest and most influential cinema semiology books. It has three sections: the first, on Eisenstein's aesthetic; the second, on auteur theory; and the third, on the semiology of the cinema. The concept of the sign is the unifying factor in the book and all sections are concerned with semiological considerations. Wollen writes clearly, has a number of "stills" from films, and offers an excellent introduction to film semiology.

Worth, Sol. *Studying Visual Communication.* (Edited, with an introduction, by Larry Gross.) Philadelphia: University of Pennsylvania Press, 1981. A valuable collection of essays by the late Sol Worth that focuses primarily on film, but also deals with other aspects of visual communications. The book contains an introduction by Larry Gross which deals with Worth's contributions as a firm maker and communications theorist.

Wright, Will. *Sixguns and Society: A Structural Study of the Western.* Berkeley: University of California Press, 1975. Wright's analysis of the western suggests that there are four basic western plots: the classical plot, the vengeance variation, the transition theme, and the professional plot. What is most interesting, for Wright, is that, as he puts it, "the Western represents forms of actions and understanding that are inherent in the changing economic institutions of America..." Wright finds important ideological content in the western myth which he uses structural analysis to uncover. A controversial and fascinating book.

There are a number of periodicals devoted to semiotics and related concerns such as *Semiotext, Semiotica, Versus, Critical Inquiry, Poetics Today* and *The American Journal of Semiotics.*

Dictionary of Concepts

Arbitrary The relationship between the signifier (or sound-image) and signified (or concept) is a matter of convention and is not natural or "motivated." There is some disagreement about this view, which was held by Saussure. Followers of Peirce believe that in some cases signs are not arbitrary.

Code A system of conventions that enables one to detect meaning in signs (in other words, permits "decoding" them). Since the relationship between sound-images and concepts is (at least in many cases) arbitrary, we need to know the codes that tell us what signs mean. For some scholars, the matter of learning or discovering codes is the central business of semiology.

Connotation For Eco, connotation is a form of signification that relies on a primary code to be understood. For Barthes connotation is, approximately, "myth," the hidden or latent ideological content attached to many signs. Conventionally connotation involves meanings and associations connected with concepts or objects. Thus the connotated meanings of champagne are luxury, happiness, celebration, and so on.

Denotation This term refers to the direct and specific (or most literal) meaning of a sign. Thus the denotated meaning of champagne would be "a sparkling white wine from the Champagne region of France."

Icon   In Peirce's system, the icon is a sign that functions by resembling its object . . . or being similar to it. A photograph of a person is an icon. The relationship between an icon and its object is not arbitrary for Peirce.

Index   In Peirce's system, the index is a sign that is causally connected to its object (and also not arbitrarily related). Thus smoke would be an index of fire; the smoke is caused by the fire and points to the existence of the fire. A great deal of our knowledge of things is indirect and indexical.

Language   Language is a social institution, "a system of signs that expresses ideas" (for Saussure) based on conventional rules. *The Random House Dictionary of the English Language: The Unabridged Edition* defines language as "any system of formalized symbols, signs, gestures, or the like, used or conceived as a means of communicating thought, emotion, etc." The notion that film, television programs, and other cultural phenomena are like languages in many respects is central to semiological analysis.

Latent   This term refers to the hidden meaning of something. . . a meaning that is not perceived, which one is not conscious of, which is generally unrecognized. When the latent meaning of some phenomenon or the latent function of some activity is discovered, it becomes "manifest."

Manifest   This term refers to the obvious, intended, recognized aspects of some phenomenon, the conscious reason for which something is done. The manifest content of a dream, for example, would be what happened in the dream. The latent content would be what the dream meant. . . which would have to be discovered by interpreting the signs and symbols in the dream.

Meaning   It is generally held that the purpose of semiotic analysis is to uncover the meaning of signs. A crucial aspect of the enterprise is recognizing that meaning is not something a sign has by itself; rather, meaning stems from relationships, from the context in which the sign is found. . . or from the system in which it is embedded. As Saussure put it, "signs function, then, not through their intrinsic value but through their relative position," or "in language there are only differences." Nothing, then, has meaning in itself. A given sign can have all kinds of different meanings, depending on the system of signs or context in which it the sign is located.

Motivated   A relationship between a signifier and signified or sign and its object is motivated if it is not arbitrary or purely conventional.

Myth   Myth is a complicated term that is used in different ways by different scholars in different disciplines. In semiotic discourse, Roland Barthes sees myth as essentially an ideological phenomenon. . . as the ideological baggage that is attached to signs (which people are not aware of, generally speaking). Lévi-Strauss studied myths to determine how the human mind functions and offers ways of interpreting and understanding myths. Myth, here, is not defined as "error" or "mistaken ideas," as myth is conventionally understood.

Semiology   Semiology is the science of signs which, for Saussure, "studies the life of signs within society." It is based on his notion of signs being composed of signifiers and signifieds and deals with what signs are, what laws govern them, and how they can be applied to arts, rites, and all manner of cultural phenomena. Semiological analysis is associated with the Saussurean perspective.

Semiotics   Semiotics is the system of sign analysis associated with C. S. Peirce that focuses on the iconic, indexical, and symbolic attributes of signs. As Peirce wrote, "It seems a strange thing, when one comes to ponder over it, that a sign should leave its interpreter to supply part of its meaning: but the explanation of the phenomenon lies in the fact that the entire universe. . . the universe which we are all accustomed to refer to as 'the truth'—that all this universe is perfused with signs, if it is not composed exclusively of signs."

Sign   The sign is a central concept in semiology and semiotic analysis. For Saussure, a sign is a "combination of a concept and sound-image." The linguistic sign, said Saussure, "unites not a thing and a name but a concept and a sound-image." For Peirce, a sign is "something which stands to somebody for something in some respect or capacity." For Eco, a "sign is everything which can be taken as significantly substituting for something else," on the basis of a previously established social convention.

Signified   The signified is the concept part of the sign, according to Saussure.

Signifier   The signifier is the sound-image part of the sign for Saussure. A sign for Saussure is both a signifier and signified; they are like two sides of a piece of paper and are always found together.

Structuralism   According to Philip Pettit, in *The Concept of Structuralism*, "Structuralism is the movement of thought which presses and formulates the case for semiology, usually at the conceptual level but also in attempts at empirical analysis. Roughly speaking, the terms are interchangeable." Terrence Hawkes suggests, in *Structuralism and Semiotics*, that central to structuralism is the notion that "the world is made of relationships rather than things," a concept found in Saussure and used in linguistic analysis. Some have suggested that what we used to call structuralism we now call semiology or semiotics. For our purposes we shall consider all three terms to be the same.

Symbol   For Saussure a quasi-natural, not completely arbitrary or motivated form of sign. For Peirce, a form of sign based on convention. It
should be pointed out that for Peirce, a sign can be iconic, indexical,
and symbolic, all at the same time. In other words, one aspect of a sign
does not preclude other aspects.

Index

Advertising, 148–154
  "Reach Out and Touch Someone,"
    151–154
  signs, 24–25
Allen, Woody, quoted 73–74
Arbitrary
  nature of sign, 10
  symbols, 19
Arcimboldo, 130–132
Arlen, Michael, 151
Auteur theory, 109, 111–113

Barthes, Roland, quoted 2–3, quoted
  21–23, quoted 27, quoted 49, 50,
  119
Baseball, 162–164
Becker, Howard, quoted 120
Berger, John, quoted 120–121
Berson, Henri, quoted 73
Bernstein, Basil, 160–161

Boggs, Joseph M., quoted 111–112
Bourdieu, Pierre, quoted 166–167

Campbell, R. J., quoted 90
Carter, David E., quoted 101–102
Cartooning, 14, 136–138
Cawelti, John, quoted 85, 86
Chase, Marilyn, quoted 98
Chicago, Judy, 38–41
Circumcision, 14–15
Clutter, 42
Codes
  aesthetic, 158, 160
  clarity in, 167
  coherence in, 165–166
  and communication, 169
  confusion, 42–43
  concreteness in, 167
  continuity in, 168
  covertness in, 166–167

definition, 189
elaborated, 160–161
levels, 158
logical, 158
restricted, 160–161
social, 158, 160–161
Color, 33–34
Connotation, 48–50, 189
Comic strips, 51–56
Contrast, 36
Coward, Rosalind, quoted 48–49
Culture codes, 156–157
Crumb, Robert, quoted 55
Crusoe, Robinson, 143–147
Culler, Jonathan, quoted 173, 175

Defamiliarization, 130–131
Demara, Ferdinand Waldo, 70
Denims, 80–82
Denotation, 48–50, 189
Descriptions, verbal, 57–58
Design, 110
Dichter, Ernest, quoted 29
Digital watches, 29–32
Dostoyevsky, Fyodor, quoted 57
Dreams
defined, 58
and fairy tables, 63–66
Droodles, 13–14

Eco, Umberto, quoted 4, quoted 43,
quoted 67, quoted 90
Eliade, Mircea, quoted 125–126,
quoted 143
Ellis, John, quoted 48–49
Emerson, Ralph Waldo, quoted 125
Ezekiel, quoted 60–61

Fashion, 80–82
Figure-Ground, 128
Food, 170–172
status and, 171–172
Ford, John, 113
Formulas
in arts, 85–88
in public art forms, 86
Freud, Sigmund, quoted 36, quoted 63,
65–66

Geertz, Clifford, quoted 20
Goffman, Erving, quoted 99
Gookin, R. Burt, quoted 100
Gorney, Roderick, quoted 69
Grain, 37
Gray, Harold, quoted 54
Green, S. A., quoted 45, 46

Hallucinations, 59
Hair
blondes, 68–69
as a sign, 97
Hawks, Howard, 113
Herriman, George, quoted 54
Hinckley, John, 90–91
Hinsie, Leland, quoted 90
Hiyano, David M., quoted 27
Hobbes, Thomas, quoted 72
Holmes, Sherlock
Blue Carbuncle, 16–18
Study in Scarlet, 157
Honor, 5–8
Humor
parody, 71–74
techniques of, 72
theories of, 72–73

Icon, 12–14, 115, 190
Identity
corporate, 24–25, 100–102
personal, 95–100, 102–103
Illusions
figure-ground, 128
Levi's ad, 128–129
optical, 127–129
Image, 75, 118
Index, 12, 190
Insignia, 110
Isaiah, quoted 94

Journal of Communication, 14, 136

Klapp, Orrin E., quoted 78, quoted 95

Language, 3
and myth, 49
definition, 190
Latent meanings, 139–142, 190

Life-style, 75–79
Lucas, George, 107

Manifest meanings, 139–142, 190
Marmer, Nancy, quoted 46
Martin, Bernice, quoted 77
Material culture, 25–27
  digital watches, 29–32
  soul in objects, 29
Meaning, 173–176
  change, 43
  and concepts, 173
  definition of, 190
  and differences, 173
  latent, 139–142
  manifest, 139–142
  and oppositions, 173–176
Mehrabian, Albert, quoted 34, 36
Metaphor, 94, 134
Milgram, Stanley, quoted 121
Morley, Jeff, quoted 98
Motivation, 190
Mueller, Claus, quoted 161
Myth, 48–49, 190
  in *Robinson Crusoe*, 144–147

Natural look, 124–126
Nature, 124–126, 144–147
Nowell-Smith, Geoffrey, quoted 109

Ogden, C. K., quoted 174–175
Oppositions
  and Aristotle, 174–175
  important, 175–176
  Jacobson on, 173
  in *The Paper Chase*, 180
  in *Return of the Jedi*, 106
  in *Upstairs, Downstairs*, 174

Pac Man, 141–142
Paper Chase, 177–180
  oppositions in, 180
Parody, 71–74
Paz, Octavio, 170–171
Peirce, Charles Sanders, quoted 1,
    quoted 12, quoted 89, quoted 191
Perkins, V. F., quoted 112
Photography, 119–121

Poetry, as sign, 92–94
Pop Art, 45–47
Price, Roger, 13
Punks, 76–79

Ray, Nicholas, 112–113
"Reach Out and Touch Someone,"
    151–154
Reagan, Ronald, 91
Resign, 109
Return of the Jedi, 104–107
Rublowsky, John, quoted 46–47

Sapirstein, Milton, quoted 26
Saussure, Ferdinand de, quoted 3–4,
    quoted 9, 10, 12, quoted 13, quoted
    19, quoted 173
Schizophrenic, hebephrenic, 90
Shakespeare, William, quoted 5–8
Shape, 36
Shkloveky, Victor, quoted 131
Signals, 20
Signature, 109
  directorial, 111–113
Signemes, 114
Signified, 9–10
  and ambiguity, 44
  and cartoons, 137
  defined, 191
  and lifestyle, 76
  and professions, 89–91
Signifier, 9–10
  and ambiguity, 44
  and cartoons, 137
  defined, 191
  and lifestyle, 75–79
  and professions, 89–91
Significant, 110
Signs
  ambiguity in, 43–44
  arbitrary nature of, 10, 13, 189
  assemblage, 115
  closure, 83–84
  cocktail, 140–141
  complex, 114–115
  construction, 83–84
  definition of, 1–4, 9–15, 24
  and food, 170–172

iconic, 134
and identity, 95–103
imaginary, 57–61
that lie, 67–70
manifest meanings, 139–142
modifiers, 133–135
no sign as sign, 122–123
systems, 148–150
and poetry, 92–94
Simile, 94
Size, 34
Sontag, Susan, 119
Spatiality, 34, 36
Structuralism, 191
Symbol, 12, 19, 20, 134
  definition of, 192

phallic, 36

Texts, 115

Upstairs, Downstairs, 174

Visions, 59–61

Watt, Ian, quoted 144
White, Donald K., quoted 97
Winick, Charles, quoted 68–69
Wolfe, Tom, quoted 34
Wollen, Peter, quoted 113
Wrestling as theatre, 2–3

Zettl, Herbert, quoted 3